His Life Our Pattern

Clarence W. Cranford

His Life
Our Pattern

BROADMAN PRESS
Nashville, Tennessee

Library of Congress catalog card number: 60–9528

Printed in the United States of America

5.JN60K.S.P.

To

the memory of my parents, who first taught me;
the memory of the pastor who early in my life asked me;
my wife, whose example daily inspires me;
my son and daughter, who as children of a Christian
father have a right to expect me;
and all who have in any way helped me

To make His life my pattern,

I gratefully dedicate this book.

Preface

IT IS A TERRIFYING experience to be lost. A child sobs convulsively in a crowd because it is lost from its mother. A hunter wanders lost through a trackless forest, looking desperately for some familiar landmark, trying to judge his position by the sun. A motorist sits baffled by an unfamiliar fork in the road, not knowing which way to take. He needs a map or the help of someone who knows the way and can guide him.

In many ways the world today is lost in a maze of fear and confusion. With all our vast knowledge, we are a crazy, mixed-up world. We know so much, and yet so little. We strive to control nature, but by lurid advertising, the exploitation of violence and sex in much of current literature and in the entertainment world, the promotion and sale of alcohol, and international name-calling we try to bring out the worst in human nature. We know how to split atoms, but cannot unite a split world. We can send satellites into outer space beyond the pull of the earth's gravitation, but cannot get the cause of peace beyond the pull of man's pride and selfish ambitions so that the nations of the world can orbit in a pattern of understanding and good will.

No wonder so many people are confused. The church, and often the home, presents one set of standards and ideals; the theater and television often present quite another. Civilization has reached a fork in the road it has never faced before.

The alternative now is nations united in peace or atomic destruction. Which will provide the map for the future—Christianity, secularism, or communism? Whose life will be our pattern—Jesus, Lenin, or some other?

It is the conviction of this book that Christ, and Christ only, must be our pattern if life is to be free and civilization worth preserving. He, and he only, fully knows the way from God and to God. He has walked the way into our humanity and our deepest needs. He has walked unscathed through the world's temptations and hates. He has walked through rejection and pain to victory over death. He comes to us now not as a mere historic personality, but as a living Person.

These chapters are based on incidents in the life of Jesus or insights from his amazing teachings. But we do not stop there. Each message tries to lead us to a point of decision. Christianity is not an escape, but a commitment. It is not—to repeat a sign seen on a church bulletin board—a "hitching post," but a "guide-post." It demands a response. It calls for faith and action. It says, "This is the way, walk ye in it."

I would express deep appreciation to members of the Calvary Baptist Church, Washington, D.C., who listened to these messages with such helpful attention, and to Miss Evelyn Baumgartner, who typed them. I sincerely hope these messages may help others to sense the urgency and see some of the ways of making "his life our pattern."

Contents

1

The Eternal Word

MATTHEW 24:35

IN HIS BOOK *The Diary of a Country Priest* Georges Bernanos says: "If only the good God would open my eyes and
unseal my ears, so that I might behold the face of my parish.
. . . The look in the eyes . . . those would be the eyes of all
Christianity, of all parishes—perhaps of the poor human race
itself. Our Lord saw them from the Cross." [1]

I, too, am haunted by the faces of people. As I stand in my
pulpit and look into the faces of my congregation, I am conscious of the needs they represent. Here are people buffeted
by life, confused by fast-changing events, often unable to
cope with their own inner urges and drives, looking for guidance and peace, grace and pardon. Where can they find the
guidance they need and desire? Where can they find that
which will give them stability and strength in the face of
temptations and trials?

On the pulpit in front of me as I preach there is a large
open Bible. Its very presence there is reassuring, like an
anchor in the time of storm. Whether they read it or not, the
people believe that this book has a message they need to
hear, that this message will throw light on their own needs

---

[1] Georges Bernanos, *The Diary of a Country Priest* (London: The Religious Book Club, n.d.), pp. 37–38.

1

and problems. But why does the Bible give such assurance? Why, in a world that is changing so rapidly, do we still go back for our moral and spiritual guidance to what was written so long ago?

We don't do that in science. Textbooks on science often are outmoded within a decade after they are written. We certainly don't do it in medicine. One would hardly submit to surgery if he were informed that the doctor was practicing medicine on the basis of what had been written about medical science fifty years ago. Why, then, do we do it in religion?

For this is a changing world. One way we know that is to think of the things commonplace today that were unknown fifty years ago. Fifty years ago people had never heard a radio, to say nothing of talking movies and television. They knew nothing about jet planes or nuclear energy. They knew nothing about transistors, tranquilizers, and traffic jams. Armadas in the sky were the pipe dream of a Tennyson or a Jules Verne. The atom to them was something that could not be split, since it was considered to be the irreducible minimum of matter.

They never heard of a "sputnik," followed by a "mutnik" and a "lunik," although they did know something about the "old Nick." Russia and America seemed a million miles apart in their world, and if they ever heard the word "communism," the chances are they never gave it a second thought. They never heard of man-made satellites or guided missiles. They never heard of penicillin or antibiotics. They never heard of Deepfreezes and ready mixes. They never even heard of Kleenex or Scotch tape. So one might ask facetiously, How did they manage to live back there, anyhow?

This is not a bad question to ask. For many of them lived very full and happy lives; they were much more contented with what they had than most people seem to be today. We ask how they were happy and content without so many of the gadgets and laborsaving devices we think are indispensable to our comfort and progress. The question reminds us that even in a changing world some things do not change. Styles change. Devices change. Motives do not. Love is still love whether we call it "spooning" or "pitching woo." Greed and lust are the same in every age. Sin is sin whether we see it exemplified in Herod or Hitler, and the results of sin have not changed one bit since Paul wrote, "The wages of sin is death" (Rom. 6:23).

Man's need for God does not change. We no longer build a tower of Babel to try to reach God. We are not that primitively naïve. Now we build launching pads for space missiles and think we no longer need God. But just as the builders of the tower of Babel could not reach God by such means, neither can we dismiss God because we know how to shoot a nose cone into outer space.

All our efforts to probe the immensities of outer space, the intricacies of the atom, and the complexities of our own inner nature are puny compared to the vastness of the mysteries we seek to understand and control. Our reason can go only so far. Our goodness is not good enough. The scene changes, but the plot remains the same: proud man seeking to control nature but unable to control himself, patient God seeking to redeem human nature by giving himself—man the sinner, God the Creator, Judge, and Redeemer. Science can give the world a "new look," but our problem is still the "old Adam." It is not guided missiles we need so much as guided men. And where does man get this guidance he needs? The Bible points to God. He is the Creator and Sustainer of life. He is the Judge of the universe. He is the One whose thinking planned it, whose laws govern it, and whose love can redeem it.

The Bible is not concerned with how fast we can travel. It wants to know where we are going. It is not concerned with what we know about science, as important as that may be. It wants to know what we know about God and what difference that knowledge makes in how we live with ourselves and with each other. It points to moral laws that cannot be repealed, to prophetic voices that announce God's purposes in history, and to a life giving itself on a cross. It echoes Christ's words, "Heaven and earth shall pass away, but my words shall not pass away" (Matt. 24:35).

A young girl once said to me, "I'd read the Bible more if it were as interesting as the *Reader's Digest*." Of course, she had not lived very long—or deeply. When she faces what someone has called "the triple tragedy of sin, suffering, and death," she will need more than the gleanings of a monthly magazine from which to draw comfort and strength. She will need the assurance of the prophet: "Though your sins be as scarlet, they shall be as white as snow" (Isa. 1:18). She will need the faith of the psalmist: "The Lord is my shepherd; I shall not want" (Psalm 23:1). She will need the comforting words of the Master: "Let not your heart be troubled: ye believe in God, believe also in me" (John 14:1).

The tragedy is that so few people read the Bible any more. I once went to speak in a New England town. Arriving early in the day for an evening engagement, I was asked if I would broadcast a morning devotional message from a local radio station. I gladly consented and broadcast a brief message on the Bible.

That evening, after I had spoken in a local church, I was approached by a man who told me this incident. He said he had gone home as usual that day for lunch. When he entered the room where his wife was seated, she was reading the Bible. Surprised to the point of being startled, he asked,

"What's the matter, dear?" She replied: "Nothing's the matter. I just heard a broadcast about the Bible, and it made me want to read it again." The man continued, "We decided at lunch that something was very much the matter in our home when we had so neglected Bible reading that when one of us saw the other with a Bible he thought something must be wrong."

Something is the matter when we do not read the Bible, for without its message we lose our greatest reason for believing in the abiding nature of moral law and purpose in life.

No one would deny that some things are wrong with our nation. The exposures of widespread corruption in labor unions, the extent of deception and dishonesty in certain TV quiz programs, the flagrant portrayal of sex and violence on our newsstands and in the entertainment world—all these have shocked decent people beyond measure. Something is wrong with the moral and ethical sensibilities of millions of people, many of them in positions of trusted leadership. There seems to be so little sense of responsibility to maintain moral standards, so little sense of sinning against society or God. The only criterion seems to be, "Can I get away with it?" The teachings of the Bible are unknown or ignored. Yet here is the book that can tell us what is wrong with us and our world. It knows what happens when men disregard and deny God. It knows the happiness and peace that faith in him can give.

Dr. Carl Sumner Knopf says that every generation is like a freshman class in chemistry. In front of the students are the chemicals and gadgets with which they are to work. The students are given also a textbook and a notebook. The teacher says: "Study the textbook. Learn what men have discovered about chemical reactions. They did not invent these reactions. They discovered them to be true. When you have learned these tested formulae, perform your experiments in the light of them, and write the results in your notebook."

One freshman gets bumptious. He says to himself, "Who wants to follow the textbook all the time?" He begins to wonder what would happen if he were to mix together a number of chemicals whose properties he does not yet know. One day when he thinks the teacher is not looking, he begins to mix together a lot of chemicals to see what will happen, and Dr. Knopf says it happens. When the experiment comes down from the ceiling, the freshman does not have to write the result in his notebook. The stain on the notebook is the result of that particular experiment.

One day a psalmist—tradition says it was David himself —experimented with faith, and the result is beautifully recorded: "The Lord is my shepherd; I shall not want" (Psalm 23:1). But another day David thought the great Teacher of the universe was not looking; so he experimented in wife-stealing and murder, and the experiment exploded on him. No one tried to hide the stain because it was David who was involved. There it is spread all across the eleventh and twelfth chapters of 2 Samuel. Even a king cannot break the laws of God with impunity.

We, like Joshua, need to go back and read again "the blessings and cursings" of the law (Josh. 8:34). We need to prescribe for our day huge doses of the Hebrew prophets. They not only spoke of the goodness of God but warned of the anger of God. History has backed up their message. They boldly proclaimed that a righteous God will not continue to bless an unrighteous people. If the Old Testament is right, there is a justice in this universe more to be feared than the probings of any congressional investigating committee.

The New Testament also warns of the judgments of God. "Knowing therefore the terror of the Lord," wrote Paul, "we persuade men" (2 Cor. 5:11). But it goes further. It reveals a grace that will heal our lives and our land if we will let it. It is not enough to trust in bombs. We must trust in the Bible and its message if we want to be led in the ways of understanding and peace.

Again, something is the matter when we do not read the Bible, for without its message we lose our greatest reason for believing in the abiding dignity and worth of man.

So much of life is lived at an impersonal level. Communism echoes Marx's contention that man is a machine that obeys exact mechanical laws. Cities engulf the individual in the crowd and make him one of the "faceless millions." Automatic machines do much of his work and computing for him with greater speed and output than he could possibly match.

A current joke tells of a professor who informed his pupils he would be absent from class on a certain day, but he instructed them to attend since he had recorded his lecture and had arranged for a student to play the recording. To take the roll, he rigged a hidden camera and timed it to snap a picture of the room during the class period. When he returned to the campus and developed the negative, he found he had a picture of a room full of tape recorders recording his recorded lecture.

What better picture can we find of the logical outcome of the present trend toward automation and impersonalization, especially if man loses his faith in the reality of God? Without a belief in God and a concept of man as a living soul made in the image of God, man becomes little more than an animated tape recorder. Take away faith in the dignity and worth of man as a child of God, and one takes away the greatest hindrance to tyranny and cruelty. If man is a child of God, rather than merely a creature of the state, tyrants have no right to abridge his freedoms without compunction. But man is not just the product of magnetized atoms. The Bible presents him as the creation of God's hand and the object of God's love. This is what gives him his dignity and worth.

Most of all, this is wrong when we do not read the Bible. Without its message we lose the unfolding record of man's reaching out in his limited way after God and God's reaching out in his infinite love after man.

Think of the scope of the Bible. The story begins in a primitive world where people believed in many gods and believed them to be whimsical and vindictive. Then God raised up a nation to declare that there is one God and that he is righteous. "Shall not the Judge of all the earth do right?" asked Abraham, and his words were an affirmation of faith, not just a question. Amos was inspired to spell out the implications of God's justice in terms of the social evils of his day. Hosea, through his tragic personal experience of loving an unfaithful wife, was led to sense something of God's love for Israel. Jonah was made to see that God's love extends even to the enemies of Israel in Nineveh.

But what is God's love like? The prophets tried to draw a picture of it. Jeremiah pictured God as the divine Potter who remakes the marred vessel. Isaiah drew a picture of the Suffering Servant. But men still missed the point. And then one day the picture took on flesh. Men did not have to guess any more what the love of God is like. Now they could see it in a life—on a cross. Dr. Walter Denny says that one cannot look at that sublime moment when Jesus prayed for his enemies from the cross without realizing that the universe that could produce such a life and such a moment has at its heart an inexhaustible well of forgiveness.

The Bible, then, takes on its supreme significance because it brings us face to face with God's act of redemptive love in Jesus. The Old Testament looks for his coming. The new Testament presents and interprets him. From the ministry of John the Baptist to the vision of John the revealer the New Testament points us to Jesus as "the Lamb of God, which taketh away the sin of the world" (John 1:29).

Once when I was lost, I asked a man how to find my way to the next town. He did not give me a set of directions. He said: "That's where I live. Follow me, and I'll lead you to it." The Bible does not present a set of rules and say, "Obey these, and you will inherit eternal life." It points us to Jesus and says, "Follow him, and he will lead you into the presence of the Father." He came from the Father. He returned to the Father. Let us, then, through the chapters of this book look to Jesus, beginning at Bethlehem and ending at an empty tomb in Arimathea's garden, that he may give us guidance and strength to run with patience the race that is set before us.

2

Stars and Stables

MATTHEW 2:1–2; LUKE 2:12

THE STORIES of the birth of Jesus as told by Matthew and Luke stand out, by their sheer beauty, as two of the greatest passages in all literature. But they are infinitely more than literature. The stories of the birth of Jesus mean more to a Christian than Beethoven's *Fifth Symphony* could ever possibly mean to a lover of music or a Rembrandt painting could mean to a lover of art, for they introduce the life of the person whose coming into the world is the very basis of a Christian's faith and hope. One can be enthralled by music or enjoy a painting without being morally changed, but he cannot follow Jesus without submitting his life to the scrutiny of Almighty God. One can take art or leave it, but he can ignore Jesus only to his own soul's peril.

What Christian, therefore, can read the stories of the birth of Jesus without a deepening sense of gratitude and joy? What a matchless life they introduce! What a story of God's unfolding love they begin to tell! How they have filled our imagination and enriched our art! What faith and hope would be snuffed out were it not for the record that begins, "Now when Jesus was born in Bethlehem of Judaea. . . ."

And what an interesting combination these stories present. The Christ child born in a stable! The wise men following a star! Here in the one great event of Jesus' birth are combined the shine of a star and the straw of a stable. Here in one sharp focus are brought together the world of the far and the world of the near, the reach of immensity and the touch of simplicity, the realm of the heavens and the region of the humble. Here we look up to see a star. Here we stoop down to enter a stable. It is almost as if the Christmas story were saying to us, Never become so earth-bound you cannot look up to see a star; never become so proud and haughty you cannot stoop to enter a stable. Thus we are reminded that two of the facets of the Christian life are divine guidance and a call to humble service—a light from above and a commission to enter life's lowliest areas to serve in the name of the lowly Galilean. And it is important that both aspects be present.

Let us look at these two features of the Christian truth. First, let us look at the star. We know a great deal more about stars today than people did in Jesus' day. We know, for example, that the earth weighs about six sextillion tons, but that a star like Canis Major weighs forty million times that much. We know the distance from the earth to the sun. We can measure celestial distances in terms of light years. But while we have more scientific information about the stars, are we any wiser? Have we not tended to lose a sense of awe and wonder at the vast extent of the heavens? We no longer think of the moon as an object of delight for poets and lovers. Now it has become a target for rockets and spaceships. Job could sing the praises of God as he looked at the stars. We think of the achievements of man as we measure their orbits. Amos was reminded of the hand of God as he sat by his sheep and watched Orion and the Pleiades. We think of the advances of science as we sit by our telescopes and photograph the Milky Way. The psalmist sang, "The heavens declare the glory of God." Our headlines read, "Scientists shoot new planet into outer space."

But man's need for God is as great as ever. When Miss Suzanne Rinck of the Baptist Missionary Training School in Chicago was sightseeing in Washington, D.C., a guide asked her what she did. She replied that she taught Bible in a Christian school. The guide said: "Pretty soon man will reach the moon. What will you do with your Bible then?"

What a question to ask! What if man does reach the moon? He will still have gone a very little distance into God's vast universe. He will still be, to quote Walter Sullivan, science writer for the *New York Times*, like "a potato bug in a sack of potatoes in the hold of a great ship, wondering what makes the ship go," with little or no knowledge of the vast world in which the ship can travel. Man will still get hungry and need food. He will still get lonely and need companionship. He will still be a sinner and need forgiveness. He will still die and need the assurance of everlasting life. He must still, if he is wise, look at the stars and ask, "When I consider thy heavens, the work of thy fingers, the moon and the stars, which thou hast ordained; what is man that thou art mindful of him?"

The wise men who sought the child Jesus were students of the stars. They, too, studied the heavens. But they saw stars as the handiwork of God and believed that one day by this very means God would give them a sign that would lead them to his greatest gift for the world. When the sign appeared, they followed it, so that whatever the star of Bethlehem was, meteor or vision, it was for them an act of God's guidance that led them to Jesus. Thus, the star of Bethlehem continues to shine in the orbit of faith as a symbol of God's love and guidance as he seeks to lead us into the presence and service of his Son.

Many people are able to conceive of God out among the stars. Even those who are primarily scientifically minded believe there must be a cosmic Mind to explain the creation and operation of the universe. Many people, however, find it difficult to believe that the God who fashions the stars and charts their courses knows or cares about us as persons and is concerned about what happens to us in this chaotic world in which we live. Many find it difficult to believe that the God of the universe is interested in each individual or that he can and will give us guidance for our personal lives.

And yet this is precisely the witness of the great saints of the ages. Even humbler folk who have sought God's guidance have experienced what Thomas Kelly called "the welling-up whispers of divine guidance and love and presence" that lead us to know "what to do and what to let alone." Often when they have sought God's guidance and have acted in faith on whatever sense of guidance they felt they have received, seekers have had their faith strengthened and have come to believe that what has happened in their lives cannot be explained as mere coincidence. Surely a Love greater than their own responded to their need, and a Will wiser than theirs guided their destinies.

God still offers guidance for our lives. He no longer uses a star to lead people to Jesus. He doesn't need to. Now he usually does it by the witness of other Christians. Now he guides us by the teachings of the Bible. Now he guides us by the witness of the church. He still invites our prayers and guides us by the still, small voice of conscience sensitized by Christian teachings. It was not a great voice that attracted the wise men's attention, but a silent star. They might not have seen it when it appeared if they had not been looking for it. God does not shout at us. He asks us to be still and know that he is God. He asks us to look at Jesus lifted up upon a cross. When we do, he often plants thoughts and feelings in us that give us the assurance of his presence and guidance.

Many have discovered a sense of God's guidance through the practice of a quiet time when, after turning their thoughts to God by Bible reading and prayer, they quietly review their lives and the needs and problems of the world in the light of the life and teachings of Jesus. They notice the thoughts that come to them, especially those that come with special insistence. One Sunday school teacher used to advise her class: "Never ignore a strong hunch. It may be more than a hunch." When these thoughts lead one in the direction of Christ, when they are accepted and acted upon in his Spirit, many times people see near miracles happen in their lives, and the results of their trust and actions are evidence to them of the reality of God's guidance in their lives.

A certain minister, as he sat in a mood of prayerful meditation, found himself thinking of a member whom he had not seen for some time. It seemed to him, as he thought about this man, that he was in distress. This feeling was so strong that the minister went at once to the member's home to find the man about to take his own life. We may not all have such a psychic premonition, but we can feel God's guidance if we bring our problems to him in prayer and expose our lives to his teachings in the Bible and his Spirit in the churches. The star of Bethlehem will shine again, as through the Bible and through the church we see it as the eternal symbol of God's loving care leading us in the direction of Jesus and a Christlike life. We need only to lift our eyes to its glorious light.

But the other side of the Christian life is represented by the stable. For if the star stands for guiding light from above, the stable stands for humility and service, and the world needs these also as an evidence of God's love.

Most of us who live in cities in our mechanical age are not very familiar with stables. We are more familiar with garages. And yet millions of people still live in close proximity to stables. In many parts of the world one sees building after building in which house and stable are under one roof. Only a partition separates the people from the animals on which they depend in their work. Stables are still very much a part of people's lives. These people, for the most part, represent the great mass of the common people of our world. They are the humble people whose toil makes it possible for others to eat and live. Most of them never get their name in the papers; yet they are the ones who give a measure of stability to our world and out of whose homes often come some of our greatest leaders.

It was just such people who followed Jesus and whom he called into his service. In asking the question why Jesus called such untrained men to be his disciples, Dr. Walter Rauschenbusch suggests that one answer may be that he was initiating a new order of leadership in the world, a leadership that would serve and not exploit, and he wanted to start with men who were not spoiled by the possession of power. So much of the leadership of Jesus' day was the kind that tried to climb up on top of people to a position of lordship. Jesus wanted a leadership that would learn to know people's needs and problems and by loving service try to lift them and their burdened lives up to a new level of faith and hope.

Perhaps the nearest Jesus ever came to a direct criticism of the Roman government under which the Jewish people of his day were forced to live was to say: "Ye know that the princes of the Gentiles exercise dominion over them, and they that are great exercise authority upon them. But it shall not be so among you: but whosoever will be great among you, let him be your minister; . . . Even as the Son of man came not to be ministered unto, but to minister, and to give his life a ransom for many" (Matt. 20:25–28).

A dissatisfied member complained that his church never had any surprises in it. That criticism could never be leveled against the life of Jesus. Everything about him was a surprise. The manner of his birth was a surprise. Whoever imagined that the Saviour of the world would be born in a stable? His teachings were a constant surprise to those who heard them. His death was a stupendous surprise. Why should the Messiah of the world have to die on a cross? His resurrection was the supreme surprise of all history.

Included in the surprises of his life was the incident in which, as the Bible puts it, "knowing that . . . he was come from God, and went to God; he riseth from supper, and laid aside his garments; and took a towel, and girded himself. After that he poureth water into a bason, and began to wash the disciples' feet" (John 13:3–5). God girded with a towel! What more of a surprise can you have than that? And yet it was Jesus' way of showing how much God is interested in ordinary, humble service that is willing to stoop to the lowest need in order to lift people to a higher level. He who cannot find something of the mind of Christ even in a stable, who is not willing to stoop in humility and service to others, has never fully understood the mind of Christ, "who, being in the form of God, thought it not robbery to be equal with God: but made himself of no reputation, and took upon him the form of a servant, and was made in the likeness of men: and being found in fashion as a man, he humbled himself, and became obedient unto death, even the death of the cross" (Phil. 2:6–8).

Here, then, are two great facets of the Christian life, one

represented by a star and the other represented by a stable. The Christian life promises guidance; it also calls for humility and service. The Christian faith inspires hope; it also makes us humble. Let us, therefore, walk as one who follows a star, but is willing to serve even in a stable; as one who walks with angels, but keeps the common touch; as one who communes with God, but walks the humble ways of men. Let us never become so earth-bound we fail to look up to see God's star leading us into the presence of his Son, nor too proud and haughty to stoop in his name to the humblest service to which God may call us.

3

Deep Water for Good Fishing

LUKE 5:1–11

THE MORNING MISTS were rising from the Sea of Galilee, or, as the Romans preferred to call it, the lake of Gennesaret. The fishermen who had been out on the lake all night were beginning to bring their boats in to the shore. Already two boats had landed, and the fishermen were washing the sea-weed and debris from their nets. One of them, Simon, worked in silence. He was tired and disappointed. He had fished all night and had caught nothing, and fishing for him was not a sport, but a means of livelihood. No fish in the nets meant less bread on the table.

While he worked, a crowd was beginning to gather along the shore. This meant the Teacher was present. Since the lake shore was one of his favorite spots, people would gather early in the morning to hear him speak, before the heat of the day became oppressive and before their daily tasks claimed their attention. On this particular morning the crowd was larger than usual, so, approaching Simon, Jesus stepped into his boat and asked him if he would row out a few feet to give him a better vantage point from which to speak to the crowd. Simon did so, and Jesus addressed the people from the boat.

After he had spoken, as the crowd was beginning to disperse, Jesus suddenly turned to Simon and said, "Launch out into the deep, and let down your nets for a draught." Simon was taken by surprise. He began to remonstrate. "Master, we have fished all night and have caught nothing." But something about Jesus made one want to do his bidding. So Simon added, "Nevertheless, at thy word, I will let down the net." So, tired as he was, he pulled his boat out into the deep water and let down the net. And the result was the biggest catch of fish he ever took, so large, in fact, that he had to summon James and John; but even with their help they could not take all the fish for their boats would have sunk.

There are several things Simon might have said in response to Jesus' command to launch out into the deep. He might have said: "Who is he that he should try to tell me how to run my life and my business? After all, I'm the fisherman in this boat. I grew up on the shores of this lake. I have fished in these waters ever since I was old enough to handle a net. I know as well as any other fisherman around here when and where the fish are apt to be running. Besides that, I have just fished all night and have caught nothing. Who is he that he thinks he has the right to tell me what to do?" So Simon might have refused to respond, and if he had, he would have missed out on the biggest catch of his fisherman's life.

Or Simon might have said: "He has no right to ask this of me now. He knows I'm tired. He knows I have fished all night and have caught nothing. I want nothing more now than to go home, get some breakfast, then get some sleep so I can come out and try again later in the day. If I were rested, it might be different. If I had not failed last night, I might respond. But this is no time to ask me. What right does he have to ask me now to launch out into the deep?" So Simon might have refused to go, and if he had, he would have failed to catch the greatest number of fish he had ever taken.

Or Simon might have decided to play it coy. He might have said: "Master, that is a good idea. That is exactly what I plan to do—later." And he might have kept rowing toward the shore all the time. Thus he might have postponed his decision to do the Master's bidding, and if he had, he would have missed out on one of the greatest moments of his fisherman's career. But because he said none of these things; because, in spite of his weariness and recent disappointment, he said, "At thy word I will let down the net," the result was a catch of fish that was the talk of the seaside for many a year to come.

One hardly need point out that each of these possible reactions to Jesus' request has its counterpart in our day. There are those, for example, who fail to launch out with Christ and the church today because of their love for the world, and so they miss out on the greatest joys and most deeply satisfying faith and hope this life can offer.

When Moses led the children of Israel into the wilderness, food was scarce, the diet was limited, the future was uncertain; so the people, in a querulous mood, began to complain to Moses. "Is not this the word that we did tell thee in Egypt, saying, Let us alone, that we may serve the Egyptians? For it had been better for us to serve the Egyptians, than that we should die in the wilderness" (Ex. 14:12). Memories are short. They were forgetting that back in Egypt they could not call body or soul their own. Every bite had to be eaten under the watchful eye of the taskmaster, whose whip could descend at any time. Better a crust of bread with freedom than a full course meal in slavery. But they had forgotten the sting of the owner's lash as they cried out, "Is not this the word that we did tell thee in Egypt, saying, Let us alone?"

There are millions of people in the world today who

frankly say to Christ and his church, "Let us alone, for it is better that we should die in our sins than that we should miss out on the pleasures and promises of the world." These people make two mistakes. They overestimate the power of sin to give them pleasure. People who live only to indulge themselves with the pleasures and successes of this world usually end up dissatisfied and often in despair. Often they become bitter and disillusioned as they come to realize that what seemed so indispensable to their happiness has not fed their soul and has robbed them in the end of the very happiness they sought.

The second mistake such people make is to underestimate the joys of the Christian life. They think that Christians are people who do not have a good time in life. Sometimes there are Christians who give that impression. But a Christian should be the happiest person on the face of the earth. Whereas the pleasures of sin end in remorse and despair and offer no promise of joy in the life to come, the joys of the Christian give new happiness every time one experiences or recalls them, and they point to the heavenly joys to come.

The tragedy is that so many people try to reach out in both directions at once. They want the joys of the Christian life, but are not completely willing to forego the pleasures of sin. They are troubled sinners, but are not sufficiently committed to Christ to be happy saints. They forget that God is the author of all true pleasures, and that when one gives himself to God and joys that are consistent with a Christian conscience, he knows happiness without remorse and a joy that will never end.

Many want to trust God, but they also want the tangible support of this world's approval. They want fish, but also want the security of being tied to the shore. They want the glow, but they are not willing to "let go, and let God" become the object of their quest and obedience. So they stay in the shallows of superficial commitment. They never venture out very far in prayer, or service, or stewardship, and then wonder why they catch only minnows of satisfaction.

Thus, there are those who fail to launch out in faith with Christ and his church because they are afraid Christ will demand too much of them. It is true that being a Christian makes demands upon our lives. There are some things a Christian must give up. There are some disciplines a Christian must accept. But we all have to live in obedience to something. The person who thinks he can live his life free of all obedience is living under a tragic misapprehension. We all have what Mrs. Regina Wieman in her book *Does Your Child Obey?* calls our "have-tos." We have to obey the laws if we want to keep out of trouble. We have to obey the doctor if we want health. We have to obey our conscience if we want to live at peace with ourselves. We have to accept the disciplines of study and practice if we want to become skilled in any vocation. The important thing is to know what we must obey in order to achieve the greatest fulness in life.

For there are two kinds of obedience. There is what Mrs. Wieman calls "servile" obedience, or the "Scrooge-Hitler" kind, and there is "creative" obedience. The first is the kind demanded by a dictator; the second is the kind expected by a father. The one is a show of authority; the other is a means of guidance. When a father sends his son to school, he is not being mean. He is doing what is necessary for the child's mental growth. God asks our obedience as a father, never as a dictator. He knows what we must obey to achieve true fulness of life. Dr. James Moffatt translates Hosea 11:3–4, "I taught Ephraim to walk, holding them in my arms; with human cords I led them, I drove with a harness of love."

That's it! God uses a harness of love. We all have to wear a harness of obedience to something, but it makes all the difference in the world whether love or some other force is holding the reins. Passion can drive with a relentless hand. It can lash us into a frenzy of despair. Ambition can drive us beyond our endurance. But love drives with a considerate hand. It seeks to guide us in the direction we must go if we are to know real fulness of life.

Yet again, there are those who fail to launch out in faith with Christ and his church because they are so conscious of past failures. They have fished all night and have caught nothing. All of us are conscious of failures we would like to forget. I once listened to a very fine minister talk to young people about purity of life. I complimented him on the able way in which he presented his ideas. He said, "I have managed to live the kind of life about which I spoke to those young people, but they will never know how hard it has been." Then, in a moment of unusual candor, he confessed, "There has hardly been a day of my life when I have not had to fight to keep thoughts of sex from assuming too great a role in my thinking." I told him I was sure he was not alone in facing this problem, but I suggested he may have been handling it in the wrong way. Instead of berating himself for the times he had tried to keep his thoughts pure and had failed, I suggested he come to God each morning and say: "Lord, here is the net of my life. Fill it to overflowing with love for thyself and my fellow men." Throughout the day he could be conscious of how God was filling it. After a while he would find there was no room for unworthy thoughts to enter.

One thing I know: Whenever we do launch out in faith with Christ, he does have some wonderful surprises in store for us. This does not mean we will not suffer. This does not mean we can never fail. It does mean that when we put our lives fully at his disposal, he does fill our nets to overflowing with evidences of his love.

I own a little cottage in Maine. The cottage isn't much, but the view from it is magnificent. The property marks the highest point in Cumberland County, of which Portland is the county seat. It commands a 360-degree view. The finest view, however, cannot be seen from the roadway. One must walk behind the cottage to see the full spread of a magnificent panorama of lakes and mountains. The members of a nearby church were invited to the cottage for a hymn sing. As one woman walked behind the cottage and came upon the view, she threw up her hands in an involuntary gesture of surprise. "To think," she said, "I have lived within twenty miles of this view all my life and never knew it was here." There are millions of people today living within a decision's distance of the joys and promises of the Christian life, but they do not know them, because they refuse to walk around whatever blocks their decision to follow Christ.

How little I realized the night I said yes to Jesus that he would fill my little net so full. There has been the opportunity to serve him. There have been so many wonderful Christian friends I would never have known had I not met them through the church. There has been forgiveness for my sins, comfort for my sorrow, guidance for my ways. Added to all this is the hope of heaven to come. As Margaret Widdemer has put it,

> Who would not pray away dearest sin
> To let such service in?

The voice of Jesus is still calling, "Launch out into the deep and let down your net." We cannot have it both ways. We cannot catch fish and stay tied to the shore. We cannot claim the promises of God and not venture out upon the will of God. We cannot feed a hungry world with the empty nets of a halfhearted discipleship. The word is clear: "Launch out!" "Let down the net." If we would know a hope that cannot be purchased and a peace that cannot be measured, whatever the excuses that rush to our lips, we must be willing to say, "Nevertheless at Thy word I will let down the net."

4

A Study in Elbows and Finger Tips

MARK 5:25–34

THERE IS AN INCIDENT in the life of Jesus that could well be called a study in elbows and finger tips. Jesus was in the midst of a tremendous crowd of people. Shoulders were bumping him; elbows were prodding him as people tried to push their way close enough to see him, to hear him, and perhaps even to see him perform a miracle.

Suddenly, in the midst of that milling, jostling throng, Jesus felt a soft touch at the very hem of his garment. He felt power go out from him. Turning around in the crowd, he asked, "Who touched my clothes?" The disciples thought he must be joking. They pointed out the great number of people who were crowded up against him. But Jesus kept looking into the faces of the people. A woman nearby, embarrassed because the spotlight of public attention was falling upon her, yet knowing she could not keep silent before those wonderful, searching eyes of Jesus, spoke up and admitted that she had touched him. Then she went on to explain why. For twelve years she had suffered an issue of blood. She had spent all she had paying doctor's bills, but she was not getting any better; rather, she was getting worse.

If Jesus could not help her, no one could. But in the hope that he could help her she reached out timidly with her finger tips, barely to touch the hem of his garment.

If one was an artist, he might try to paint the face of Jesus as he must have looked when he spoke the next word. "Daughter," he said tenderly; and one can imagine that at the very tone of his voice the woman's embarrassment left her and there was left only the glory of knowing she was in the presence of Jesus. "Daughter, thy faith hath made thee whole; go in peace, and be whole of thy plague."

If we had been there, we probably would have been in that crowd. We might have been among those who pushed their way to his very side. We might have boasted about it later. "Were you there?" we might have asked. "Did you see him? I got close enough to touch him. I bumped into him. Were you there when Mrs. So-and-so touched him? You know how sick she has been lately? Tonight she says she never felt better in her life. It's strange. I touched him, but I don't feel any different; yet she touched him, and was healed. I wonder why." Thus we might have raised the question, Why, when the woman touched him, was she healed, and why, when the crowd touched him, did nothing happen? What made the difference?

One answer to this question might be that when the people in the crowd touched him, they just touched him, but when the woman touched him, she touched him out of a sense of her need.

Have you ever thought about her need? Whatever her trouble was, medically speaking, she was gradually losing her precious life's blood. Little by little, she was becoming more anemic. Every time she suffered a hemorrhage, she lost a little more of her blood. Some years ago in Nebraska, John G. Neihardt was elected by the legislature as the poet laureate of the state, becoming the first American poet to be so honored by a lawmaking body. In one of his poems he tells how he would like to die. He writes,

> 'Let me be as a tune-swept fiddle string
> That feels the Master Melody—and snaps!'

But that is not how this woman was going to die. She was dying a little bit at a time. Day by day she was growing weaker. For twelve years healthwise she had been going downhill.

Is there not a lesson in that for us to consider? Most people do not rob a bank, or commit adultery, or commit some sin so grievous it destroys their reputation overnight. But what of the little things that drain us of spiritual power a little bit at a time—things so seemingly small we tend to overlook them till we wake up some morning and wonder where our spiritual vitality has gone? Such things as lack of prayer life, love of social prestige, love of success, thoughts of lust we hardly admit even to ourselves, envy, an unforgiving spirit—these are things that can be deadly to Christian growth and joy. A dear Christian woman once asked me to pray that God would rid her life of jealousy of another woman. She knew that if it were allowed to continue it would drain her of spiritual power. And she was right to turn to prayer. It takes the same touch of the same forgiving power to dry up those little fountains of sinful desire as it takes to deal with the more obvious sins that are too big to be togged up in hypocrisy and paraded as righteousness.

But there was another difference between the way the crowd touched Jesus and the way the woman touched him. The crowd pushed its way unthinkingly into his presence; the woman, conscious of his divine power, reached out timidly to touch him with reverence. Surely it was not just fear that caused her to reach out from behind to touch the hem of his garment. If he were the Messiah, if he were sent of God, one did not rush unthinkingly into his presence. If one touched him at all, he touched him with utter reverence.

Henry T. Finck tells about a group of American tourists that some years ago visited a museum in Vienna in which one of the prized possessions was an old piano that once belonged to Beethoven. One of the party, a young American girl, asked if she might play it. The guide gave her permission. Seating herself before the historic instrument, she began to play a cheap little jazz tune that was then popular in America. As she was playing, the guide explained to the crowd that Paderewski had once visited the museum just to see this instrument. The girl was intrigued. She stopped playing and asked, "Did he play it, too?" The guide replied: "No. We had hoped he would, but he refused; he said he wasn't worthy." Here was a girl who, lacking appreciation for Beethoven's genius, had no reverence for the instrument at which he had worked, whereas Paderewski, with his great understanding of Beethoven's stature as a musician, had such reverence for the composer's piano that, though himself a great musician, he refused to touch it.

I once watched a group of young people in an old church in Trappe, Pennsylvania. The church has stood since before the days of the American Revolution. One boy walked up into the old historic pulpit and pretended he was preaching. Catching sight of one of the leaders, called affectionately by the young people "Uncle Tom," the boy called out, "Come on up, Uncle Tom." The older man shook his head. He walked to the side of the old pulpit, and, with a hand that trembled a little, he reached out in a gesture of reverence as tenderly as a mother might reach out to touch the cheek of her baby, and touched the side of the pulpit. Perhaps the youth did not know he had been rebuked.

Have we not lost a sense of reverence in the presence of the sacred things of life? We joke about love and marriage as if these were comic affairs. We stand with our hats on, à la Hollywood, in the presence of the precious things of life. We handle the Bible as if it were an ordinary book. We rush in and out of prayer so casually that sometimes we end up jostling Jesus rather than touching him.

Take the matter of worship. Here is life's most precious privilege—finite man communing with infinite God. Surely one should never enter such a relationship casually or carelessly. After all, this is the King of the universe whose presence we seek. He is our Creator. He is the one who judges our sins. He is the one whose forgiveness we seek. He is the one whose love is revealed in Christ. It is no mere person of whom we sing in the words, "The church's one foundation is Jesus Christ her Lord." This is the Son of God whose praise we proclaim. The bread and the cup of the Lord's Supper may be only symbols, but they are symbols of him, and should never, therefore, be taken carelessly. We must not rush into his presence as thoughtlessly as the crowd that milled around Jesus, but as reverently as the woman who, though hesitantly and perhaps fearfully, reached out in reverence and faith to touch the hem of his garment.

For this is the greatest difference of all between the way the crowd touched him and the way the woman touched him. The crowd just touched him, and, so far as we know, nothing happened. The woman touched him with faith, and her faith made the difference. The same power was there for the others, but it took faith to release it.

Notice that this was not the first thing in which the woman had had faith. She had had faith in medicine, and while doctors did their best, they could not help her. A seminary president used to say, "We are not saved by faith, but by the objects of our faith." "We can have faith in the wrong thing. We can have faith in our own cleverness like those whom Jesus said prayed "with themselves." The Communist has faith, sometimes fanatically so, but it is faith in that which cannot save him or the world from sin and hate.

We have faith in education, and so we should. A person would not want to live in a world without education. But education alone can never save us. An educated sinner is still a sinner. He may be more fiendishly clever than he was before. We have done more than touch the hem of science's garment. We have grabbed hold and held on for dear life, crying, "Science, save us." But while science has its uses, and its uses are very important, in the light of the potential danger from nuclear energy which science has unearthed we feel like crying, "Lord, save us from science."

Of course, our real prayer should be, "Lord, save us from ourselves." The plague is in us. Man is the sinner whose self-will thwarts the will of God. Man must come back to the source of true healing if the world is to be saved. That source is the healing love that streams from Calvary's cross. Therefore, whether it be the first or the ten thousandth time we reach out to touch him, let us come conscious of our personal need; we are so weak. Let us come in reverence; he is the Creator and Redeemer of our souls. Let us come with such faith that we, too, will again hear the gracious words, "Thy faith hath made thee whole; go in peace, and be whole of thy plague."

5

When Others Offend

MATTHEW 18:21–22

CHRISTIANS MAY NOT AGREE on what constitutes the most difficult requirement of the Christian life, but they would surely agree that one of the most difficult is the requirement to forgive. Yet the teaching is clear. If we expect forgiveness, we must be willing to grant it. If we want God to forgive us, we must at all times be willing to forgive others.

This is not easy. I was driving along in three-lane traffic when the driver alongside me speeded up and cut into my lane so sharply he almost sideswiped my front fender, and might have done so if I had not slowed my car. Any driver knows this kind of driving is difficult to forgive. As traffic slowed for a red light, I pulled into the next lane, drew alongside him, and turned to glare my resentment at him. I was so intent on glaring I failed to notice that a taxi in front of me had stopped more quickly than I thought it would; so I hit its rear bumper. Fortunately, I was going too slow to cause any damage except to my pride. Fortunately, also, the taxi driver was in a more forgiving frame of mind than I had been just the moment before. The incident served to remind me of the importance of a forgiving spirit. Whatever satisfaction I got from glaring my resentment was offset by the danger in which I put myself and others by my desire to get even.

Forgiveness is one of the most difficult requirements of the Christian life; yet Jesus insists it is one of the most necessary. He speaks of it in the Lord's Prayer and underscores its importance by adding a further explanation of it. Peter, sensing its significance in the mind of Jesus, one day asked him, "Lord, how oft shall my brother sin against me, and I forgive him? till seven times?" Magnanimous Peter! Surely once would be enough, but Peter, wanting to parade his magnanimity, suggested seven times. Jesus must have taken his breath away when he replied, "I say not unto thee, Until seven times: but, Until seventy times seven."

Seventy times seven! One might just as well say, "Seventy times seven, times seven, times seven, and on to infinity," which is evidently what Jesus meant to suggest. In other words, Jesus put no limitations on forgiveness. The spirit of forgiveness is to be as much a part of the ongoing manifestation of the Christian life as breathing is to life itself. We make room for God's love in our hearts to the extent that we are willing for them to be emptied of all hatred and bitterness toward others.

But why should we forgive? Why is it so important to forgive others? Jesus suggests, for one thing, we need to forgive others because we ourselves need so much forgiveness, and God is willing to forgive us so much. When John Wesley was in Georgia, he pleaded the case of an offending colonist before the British governor of the colony. The British governor rejected the plea by saying, "I never forgive," to which John Wesley replied, "Let us hope, then, you never offend."

But we have offended; we do offend. Almost every moment of the day we are so much less than God wants us to be. Jesus illustrates our plight with a story. A certain man owed his king ten thousand talents. That is a lot of money. In 2 Chronicles 25 we read that King Amaziah hired an army of a hundred thousand soldiers for only one hundred talents. Ten thousand talents would mean literally millions of dollars. To all intents and purposes, it would be an unpayable debt.

It certainly was for the debtor. The note came due, and he was bankrupt. All he could do was to throw himself on the mercy of his king. Fortunately for him, the king in his great mercy forgave him the huge debt. Then the man who was freed from his debt hunted up another man who owed him only one hundred pence and demanded payment. When the king heard of such gross ingratitude, he took the offender and threw him in prison, where he would spend the rest of his life trying to work out the debt the king had been willing to cancel for him.

How can we fail to forgive others, suggests Jesus, when God is willing to forgive us so much? Sometimes when we hear of someone who has done a terrible thing, we say, "Why doesn't God strike such a person down?" But where would we be if God went around striking down every person who displeased him? Where would we be if we got our just deserts? Where would we be if God were not a forgiving God, if we could not say with assurance, "He hath not dealt with us after our sins; nor rewarded us according to our iniquities"? We need to forgive because we ourselves have been forgiven so much.

But there is a deeper reason than this why we need to forgive. We need to forgive, says Jesus, that we may feel and act like children of God, who "maketh his sun to rise on the evil and on the good, and sendeth rain on the just and on the unjust" (Matt. 5:45). Why should we try to love our enemies? Because of what it will do for them? Only in part. Love is the one power that has a chance of turning an enemy into a friend. But it does not always work like that. Sometimes, in spite of our efforts to win him with love, an enemy goes right on being an enemy. Why then should we love him? Because of what it will do for him? No, but because of what it will do for us. It will keep us from acting like an enemy. It will keep us from stooping to the level of hate and revenge. It will make us feel and act like children of God.

Dr. E. Stanley Jones tells of a bishop who would dim his lights when a driver approached him from the opposite direction at night. But if the other driver did not dim his lights as quickly as the bishop thought he should, sometimes he would shine his own bright lights back into the face of the oncoming motorist. Finally, however, he decided to stop doing this and to keep his own lights dim regardless of what the other driver did, not only because it was safer, but because it made him feel more like a bishop. Forgiving others, said Jesus, helps us to feel and act more like children of God, who offers his love and forgiveness to all who need them.

But what does it mean to forgive? It does not mean just to let bygones be bygones. It does not mean we cannot be critical of other people's faults. Indeed, if one was not repelled by sin, if he could shrug it off as if it did not matter, there would be no need to forgive. We feel we must forgive the other person because we judge him to be wrong. Sometimes we may have to tell another person he is wrong, but everything depends on the spirit in which we do it. Dwight L. Moody used to say, "You may have to tell another person he is going to hell, but if you get any pleasure out of it, you yourself are not a Christian."

Forgiveness does not mean being morally neutral. If God were morally neutral, if he could treat sin as if it did not matter, the cross would not have been necessary. The cross is evidence of the seriousness with which God deals with sin. Jesus knew a righteous God could never treat sin as if it did not matter, could never merely let bygones be bygones; and so, even at the cost of Calvary, he reached out to save men from sin's awful grasp.

What, then, is forgiveness? For one thing, it is recognizing that there is much in the other person to respect and admire —something worth forgiving. I do not know who said it first —it seems to have appeared anonymously in a Marion, Kentucky, newspaper—but someone said:

> There is so much good in the worst of us,
> And so much bad in the best of us,
> That it ill behoves any of us
> To find fault with the rest of us.

And Joaquin Miller once put it:

> In men whom men condemn as ill
> I find so much of goodness still,
> In men whom men pronounce divine
>   There is so much of sin and blot,
> I do not dare to draw a line
>   Between the two, where God has not.[2]

We forgive because we find in the other person so much to be admired and in ourselves so much that needs to be forgiven.

Moreover, the spirit of love and forgiveness is the one ingredient that has a chance to change a situation for the better. There is an interesting Swedish folk tale[3] about a man who came to a house back in the country. He knocked at the door to ask shelter for the night, and a mean-faced little old

---

[2] Joaquin Miller, "In Men Whom Men Condemn," *One Thousand Quotable Poems* (Chicago: Willett, Clark and Company, 1937), p. 228.

[3] Adapted from "The Old Woman and the Tramp," *Tales of Laughter*, ed. Kate Douglas Wiggin and Nora Archibald Smith (Garden City, New York: Doubleday, Doran and Company, Inc., 1931), pp. 463 ff.

woman opened the door a crack and asked, "What do you want, tramp?" The stranger replied: "I am not a tramp. I'm a stranger far from home, and I wondered if I could spend the night sleeping on your kitchen floor where it is warm."

The woman said: "I cannot let you in. If I do, you will want food, and I am a poor woman; I have none to give you." "Then," said the stranger, "I ought to come in and share with you what I have." This intrigued the old woman, so she opened the door and said: "Come in. What do you have to share with me?" The man took a shiny nail from his pocket and said: "I can make you some nail broth. If you will get me a pan of water and put it on the stove, I will make you the most delicious nail broth." So she put a pan of water on the stove, and he dropped the nail into it.

As the water boiled, and the nail bounced merrily around in the water, he stirred it carefully and said: "Of course, it may be a little thin. Last week I made broth with this same nail for the Earl of Clivedon, but he did add a handful of meal to it." The little old woman went to the cupboard and came back with two handfuls of meal which she dropped in the water. "If the Earl of Clivedon can give one handful of meal, I can give two. What do you think of that?" The stranger said: "I think it shows what a wonderful person you are. You are so kind, I wish I could put in some beef to flavor it." "It's beef you want," said the old woman. And going to the cupboard, she came back with a few pieces of beef and dropped them into the nail broth. As he stirred it, he said, "You are such a wonderful person, I wish we had some coffee so I could toast you." "You think we have no coffee?" said the woman, and she went and got some coffee.

Soon the aroma began to fill the kitchen. Said the stranger, "I wish we had a nice tablecloth, so I could eat with such a wonderful person as you are." The woman went to an old chest, took out an old embroidered tablecloth she had not used in years, and placed it carefully on the table. She thought, "One cannot eat with such a wonderful guest in her work dress; she must have on her best gown." So she went to her room, and as she went by the window, she took a flower from a pot and put it in her hair. Soon she came back dressed in her nicest gown, and they ate the wonderful nail broth together. After the stranger had spent the night on the warm kitchen floor, he waved good-by, and she waved in return. She smiled to herself as she did so, for now she need never be poor again. She knew how to make nail broth.

Just as flattery and appreciation brought out the best in the old woman, so a genuine spirit of forgiveness is the only thing that can heal the breach when another has offended us by his attitudes or actions. For this is what forgiveness is. Essentially, it is the restoration of a broken relationship—a relationship that has been marred by some hurt or offense, real or imagined. Forgiveness means holding out a pathway of love over which a person who has offended can walk back into a restored sense of fellowship. This is what seventy times seven means. One must continue to hold out the pathway of love until the other sees it and wants to return. The one who has offended cannot by himself establish the road back. His attempt to do so runs up against our judgment and rejection of his sin. Only love that judges the sin and yet forgives it, that takes to itself the hurt and swallows its pride, can heal the breach. This, of course, is never easy. This is why the forgiver as well as the forgiven stands in need of God's help.

This is the burden of a story told in *High Wind at Noon* by Allan Knight Chalmers. Peer Holm's next door neighbor owned a vicious dog. People urged him to get rid of it lest it harm someone, but he refused to do so. One day what they feared happened. The dog attacked Peer Holm's little girl and killed her. The community was so enraged at the dog's owner that they created a boycott against him. They refused to sell him any grain to plant in his field which he had plowed and furrowed. When the wheat began to come up through the ground on other people's farms, his field was still brown, because no one would sell him a grain of wheat.

In the middle of one night Peer Holm went out to his own granary and got a sack full of wheat. Then he went next door and in the moonlight began to scatter the seed on his neighbor's field. When others discovered what he had done and asked him why, he replied, "I did it so that God could come alive again."

One way to know God is to act like him. And one way to act like him is to forgive. As we permit him to empty our own hearts of vindictiveness and hate, God's love rushes in with healing power to take their place. "After this manner therefore pray ye: . . . Forgive us our debts, *as we forgive our debtors*"—not once, not twice, but until seventy times seven.

6

"One Thing Thou Lackest"

MATTHEW 19:16–22

DR. JOHN A. BROADUS, cofounder of the Southern Baptist Theological Seminary and one of the foremost preachers and Bible scholars of his day, was a deeply religious person. Even as a student at the University of Virginia he was recognized not only for his outstanding Christian leadership, but also for his genuine concern for the spiritual welfare of others. On one occasion he was asked by one of his classmates, a young man who was a fellow student of Greek but not a professing Christian, to write something in his autograph book. Young Broadus obliged by writing in Greek, *Hen se husterei,* "One thing thou lackest." Years later he was to learn through one of his students that his former classmate had become an active Christian layman and that he gave the credit for his conversion to what John A. Broadus had written in his autograph book.

"One thing thou lackest." These words might well be written across much of our western civilization today. For, with all its scientific and technological advances, ours is an age that lacks any great faith in God. Men are no longer motivated by a deep-seated desire to do the will of God. Many would rather put their trust in missiles than in missions, in bombs rather than Bibles, in force rather than Christian

40

friendship. Much of the prevailing mood of our time is secularistic, and secularism has been defined as "practical atheism." It is not that men deny the existence of God. In fact, more people go to church than ever before. It's just that in their daily lives so many ignore him. God so often is elbowed aside to be considered only in time of dire emergency, when he is called in as a kind of "rescue squad." Like the world of Paul's day, it can be said of men today that "professing themselves to be wise" they have become "as fools" in their conduct of human affairs.

The words used with such telling effect by John A. Broadus come, of course, from Jesus' conversation with the rich young ruler who came asking, "What good thing shall I do, that I may have eternal life?" Jesus answered, "If thou wilt enter into life, keep the commandments." The young man pressed his inquiry by asking, "Which?" Whereupon Jesus named several of the Ten Commandments, to which the young man replied, "All these things have I kept from my youth up: what lack I yet?" Then Jesus, sensing the young man's selfish pride and his obvious attachment to wealth, said, "One thing thou lackest: go thy way, sell whatsoever thou hast, and give to the poor, and thou shalt have treasure in heaven: and come, take up the cross, and follow me." If any one thinks the Christian life is easy, let him read those words again. This was too much for the young man. We read, "He went away sorrowful: for he had great possessions."

Notice, in the first place, that the young man is represented as lacking only one thing, but that one thing kept him from enjoying the assurance he sought of complete acceptance with God. Some things can be lacking without much difficulty, but let us lack something really essential and it can spell the difference between victory and defeat in our lives.

An automobile, for example, can lack certain accessories,

such as seat covers or a radio, and not have its efficiency impaired in the least; but let it lack gasoline, and even though it be the highest-priced car on the market, it cannot move an inch. A home can lack luxuries. It can lack everything but the bare necessities of life, and its members can be happy; but let it lack love, and all the luxuries in the world cannot make it a home. A church can lack oratory in the pulpit, or a high-priced choir, and still carry on an effective ministry to the glory of God; but let it lack faith and loyalty on the part of its members, or let it lack an evangelistic concern, and, regardless of its other assets, it is on its way out. A person can lack education, or even refinement, and be thoroughly honest; but let him lack integrity, and all the education in the world cannot make up for that essential lack. And a person can have all the basic requirements for physical security in this world, but let him lack faith in God and he lacks the basis for the only security that can never be taken from him and that is not limited to this life.

Before asking what it was the rich young ruler lacked, let us ask what he had, for it was not what he lacked but what he had that made Jesus love him. For one thing, he had great possessions; but that is not what attracted Jesus. In fact, Jesus urged him to give away his material wealth that his true riches might become apparent. For this man had great personal winsomeness and charm. That is clear from the record, for we are told that Jesus "beholding him loved him." Not that Jesus did not love everybody, but in this young man Jesus found such evident winsomeness and charm that he was moved to instant affection for him and desired him as a disciple. The same invitation he extended to James and John Jesus also extended to the rich young ruler; only this time the invitation was rejected.

Again, this young man had a desire to inherit eternal life.

This was certainly to his credit. With all his possessions—and they are indicated as being great—he had not let his material wealth completely blind him to his spiritual needs. In fact, he seems to have felt a lack in his life that all his material possessions could not supply, or else he would not have gone— Mark says he ran—to Jesus to ask, "What good thing shall I do to have eternal life?"

Furthermore, he had a good record so far as not breaking any of the commandments was concerned. He had not robbed anyone, but evidently he had not done much to help other people either. He had not done anything morally wrong, but neither had he used his great wealth to provide more wholesome opportunities for those under his authority so that they, too, might not be so easily led to fall into temptation. He probably did not miss a worship service in his synagogue, but neither did he carry his religious principles over into his daily practices so far as helping other people was concerned. In other words, he was a perfect example of negative goodness, and in this world of suffering and sin that is not enough. The man who wrapped his talent in a napkin and buried it had done nothing wrong with it either. He had not wasted it in riotous living as the prodigal son would have done. But Jesus rebuked him, nevertheless, for failing to put it to some good use.

For, as Jesus pointed out, it is by losing our lives that we find them. Even if our quest is the good life, we miss it if we concentrate on the selfish attainment of it. This is the danger of much of the "peace of mind" emphasis we find in religion today—it is too self-centered. Peace of mind is a wonderful by-product of the Christian life, but it must not be made our only, or even our primary, goal. Only as we lose ourselves in loving service to God and our fellow men do we find the peace and joy that otherwise elude us.

What, then, did the rich young ruler lack? For one thing, he lacked a true understanding of the real nature of Jesus' message. He still thought of salvation as something that depended on what he did. "What good thing shall *I* do," he asked, "that I may have eternal life?" But our acceptance with God and our hope for eternal life do not depend on anything we can do to deserve it, but on God's willingness to give it. Salvation is not a mechanical process whereby we do this and God does that. It is a way of life based on faith in God and surrender to his will. God is not a slot machine into which we put a good deed and get out a divine blessing. He is a loving Father who asks the love of his children and who wants them, in turn, to love and serve each other. His condition for giving his love is not a special performance, but a surrendered life. Nothing the young man did, so long as his heart was selfish, could serve to win him complete acceptance with God.

A family sat down to a tasty meal. The food was set on the table. The vegetables were steaming. The meat was in place, ready to be carved. Suddenly the hostess said, "Oh, I forgot the plates." That was all they lacked—the plates. The food was there; their appetites were keen; but without plates they could not enjoy the meal. So God's love is unlimited, but without faith it is impossible to receive it. Paul said, "Eye hath not seen, nor ear heard, neither have entered into the heart of man, the things which God hath prepared for them that love him" (1 Cor. 2:9). But without faith that puts God first and evidences itself in a surrendered life, it is impossible to receive the rich spiritual gifts God has in store for us.

In the second place, the rich young ruler lacked the willingness to let go the thing that kept him from enjoying a sense of complete fellowship with God. In his case it was the love of material wealth. With us it may be something else.

Whatever it is, nothing should be allowed to pre-empt our desire to do God's will.

A child's book of animal stories tells that one way to catch monkeys is to drill a hole in a coconut shell just large enough for a monkey to put its hand through the opening. Then the coconut is partly filled with rice and attached to a tree. When a monkey feels the rice in the shell, it fills its hand too full to permit it to be withdrawn. All it has to do in order to go free is to let go of the rice, but because it is unwilling to give up its prize, it remains trapped and is captured. There is nothing more tragic in life than a person who will not let go of some earthly pursuit or pleasure that is keeping him from enjoying a sense of full acceptance with God.

When Jesus asked the rich young ruler to give up his wealth, he knew he was asking him to give up the thing he loved most of all. The young man wanted to receive God's riches, but was not willing to share his own. He wanted an inner assurance and peace, but was not willing to give up the pursuit of wealth that kept him from enjoying them. He was an island of unconcern in a vast sea of human suffering and need, and so Jesus could not give him the assurance he so earnestly sought. For God cannot live in a selfish heart. He wants a life that is ready both to receive and express his love.

Finally, because he was unwilling to surrender the thing that dulled his spiritual sensitivity, the rich young ruler lacked the joy that might have been his if he had followed Christ all the way. For we read, "He went away sorrowful: for he had great possessions." It would have cost him dearly to follow Jesus, but the cost would have been small compared to the incomparable joy of daily fellowship with the Master. For a few paltry dollars he gave up the chance to be associated with history's most glorious leader. For material considerations he gave up the chance to help launch history's greatest movement. Of course, he could not know that then. But one thing he knew. Because he lacked the courage to follow Jesus all the way, he went away sorrowful, knowing that his cowardice of soul had robbed him of his greatest chance to count for God.

It is always so when we lack the faith and courage to follow Christ's will. Often Christians are faced with community patterns that run contrary to the teachings of the Bible. Sometimes they are called upon to make a decision, to choose between standing for Christian truth or yielding to community pressures. If they yield to community pressures, they are not happy. Their joy is clouded by an uneasy conscience. Jesus says to churches as well as individuals, "Follow me." How tragic when a church chooses community approval rather than the will of Christ and goes its way unhappy in its compromise because it had great community prestige.

In the state of Colorado there is a mountain resort known as Baldpate Inn. It is well known because it boasts the largest collection of keys in the world. There are literally thousands of keys of all conceivable shapes and sizes, many of them of great historic value. But when one wants to unlock the door of his own house, the key he needs is none of these. He needs the key that fits the lock in his own door. No other will serve the purpose.

There are many keys to life's fuller values. There is the key of education that helps unlock the door to success. There is the key of wealth that helps unlock the door to prestige and power. But when it comes to the joy of experiencing a sense of complete fellowship with God, there is only one key that will suffice, and that is a surrendered life—a willingness completely to accept God's will and to follow Christ. Without Christ's presence and redeeming love we face life's greatest issues with sorrow. Without the revelation we find in him we lack the assurance we need. That is why one lacks the essential thing who is not willing to say:

> I'd rather have Jesus than silver or gold,
> I'd rather be His than have riches untold,
> I'd rather have Jesus than houses or lands,
> I'd rather be held by His nail pierced hand
> Than to be the king of a vast domain,
> > Or be held in sin's dread sway.
> I'd rather have Jesus than anything
> > This world affords today.[4]

"One thing thou lackest." These words are written across much of our twentieth-century civilization. Will they be written across our individual lives as well?

---

[4] Words by Rhea F. Miller. Copyright renewal 1950. Used by permission.

7

Lessons from a Busy Intersection

MATTHEW 21:1–9

ON PALM SUNDAY Christians around the world rejoice that at least once during his lifetime Jesus received the adoration that was his due. With what high hopes the people must have acclaimed him on that day of his triumphal entry into Jerusalem! They were so eager to welcome a leader who could throw off the yoke of Rome, and here was one who, if he were the long-awaited Messiah, would have even the powers of heaven at his command. This was the moment for which the disciples had been waiting. Perhaps now Jesus would declare himself, set up his new kingdom, and assume the throne of David. It was also the day of which the Jewish leaders were afraid. What would happen to them and to their prestige and authority if Jesus were to declare himself king of the Jews? How would Rome react to such a development? Would not Rome move in with ruthless power to crush anything that might look like a popular uprising around a new leader? These were some of the considerations that heightened the significance of the occasion and stirred the feelings of the people as Jesus rode into the city of Jerusalem.

48

But it is interesting to note that this whole wonderful occasion was made possible partly because certain unnamed persons were willing to loan Jesus the animal on which he rode. For when Jesus planned to enter the city, he first sent his disciples to a place near an important intersection outside the city of Jerusalem, between the suburbs of Bethany and Bethphage. Here they would find a colt so young it had never yet been ridden. Jesus requested them to bring the colt to him, explaining to the owners, "The Lord hath need of him."

The owners of the colt lived where two important roadways crossed, so that day by day they could see the travelers and caravans moving in and out of Jerusalem. Day by day they could see Roman soldiers moving back and forth along these highways. Sometimes they saw their neighbors being commandeered by Roman soldiers to carry their equipment a mile. Resentment and the desire for freedom must have flared up in them as they witnessed such sights as these. Yet how helpless they must have felt in the face of such oppression. How could they do anything about it, either to resist Rome or to help their own people? Often as they watched Roman centurions ride past on prancing steeds of war, their minds must have gone back to the ancient vision of Zechariah of a new kind of king who would one day come—not as a warrior, but as a servant of the people; not to impose military rule upon the people, but to lead them to freedom and peace; one who would symbolize his mission by riding not on a horse trained for battle, but on a lowly beast of burden. How often they must have longed for the fulfilment of that prophecy! How little they realized that when it came to pass, they would play a small, but significant, role in its unfolding!

It is so easy to feel frustrated as we look out at the sheer magnitude and complexities of the problems of our world.

"I'd give anything in the world if I could feel that my life could make a difference in a time like this," is the way one person expressed her sense of frustration in the face of the world's baffling problems. Nothing seems simple any more. Problems are so complex. World tensions are so great. Modern methods of warfare are so frightening. We seem so helpless to know what to do, where to turn. How we long for a leader who can lead us into the paths of peace! Our own abilities seem so inconsequential in the face of world need—as inconsequential as an ordinary donkey in the face of the Roman army. Yet even a donkey was important to Jesus' plans to declare his kingship to the world—a kingship that would outlast the marching legions of Rome.

Although the owners of the colt may not have realized it, notice, first of all, they were in a position to make an important contribution to the world on that long-ago day because they knew Jesus. Not only that, but they knew him as Master. This seems evident from the story. This was not clairvoyance on Jesus' part. Jesus and the disciples must have passed this home many times on their trips to and from Jerusalem. At some time or other Jesus must have visited with these people. He knew they had a colt, knew when it was born, knew it never yet had been ridden. Moreover, he knew the owners would be willing to let him use the animal. They would need no explanation as to who the Master was. They would need no arguments to persuade them to let him have the loan of the colt. They knew Jesus—knew him as Master—and were willing to put what they had at his disposal. Therefore, their lives were in a position to count for Jesus when he needed them and thus to make an important contribution to their world.

The minute a person lets himself be known as a Christian, his life is in a position to make a difference to those who know him, because the world expects certain things of a Christian. As surely as an overhanging rock is in a position to fall, a Christian is in a position to exert an influence for love and righteousness, for the world expects such things of a follower of Jesus.

It is always a deep tragedy when a minister of religion is guilty of scandalous conduct. His ministry is impaired, his church is hurt, his community is shocked, because people expect a minister of religion to practice what he preaches. But there is not one standard for the clergy and another for the laity. The world expects—and has a right to expect—that every Christian shall be honest. The world expects—and has a right to expect—that every Christian shall be upright in his moral and ethical dealings. Not only God, but the world, expects a Christian to be a person of prayer. The world expects a Christian to seek and do the will of God. The very fact that one declares himself as a Christian puts him in a position to exert a needed influence for righteousness in our world.

Nor did the owners of the colt have to leave their own home to be of service to the Master. Notice, in the second place, their opportunity came to them right where they were. It was at their own gate the disciples appeared asking for the loan of their animal.

So often we think that if we were someone else, or if we were a gifted person, our lives might count for Jesus and make an important contribution to our time. If we could serve in the United Nations, or if we could go out as a missionary, or if we had wealth and influence, perhaps we could do something significant for our world. Sometimes it does not occur to us that each person must make his contribution in his own way right where he is. William Carey was the first modern missionary to go halfway around the world to preach the gospel. But William Carey surrendered his life to Christ because of the influence of a fellow apprentice who worked beside him in the cobbler's shop where together they learned how to make shoes—a youth of whom Carey said, "He could not answer my questions, but I could not answer his life."

This was the message Jesus impressed on the Gadarene demoniac. After he had been cured, the man asked Jesus if he might go with him, but Jesus replied, "Go home to thy friends, and tell them how great things the Lord hath done for thee" (Mark 5:19). We cannot all go as a missionary to a foreign country, but we can show a missionary spirit in the block where we live. We cannot all win the acclaim of the world, but we can win the love and respect of our family by the way we live. We cannot all achieve greatness, but we can strive for goodness, and the world needs goodness more than it needs greatness. There is something that each of us can do.

Finally, the owners of the colt were able to assist the cause of Jesus, and thus help to bring his message to the world, because they had what the Master needed at the time. What they had was only a donkey, but that is exactly what Jesus needed on that particular day. Jesus knew the way Zechariah had pictured the Messiah would come. Moreover, the people were familiar with this prophecy. If Jesus came riding on a donkey, the people would make the connection and know that thus he was symbolizing his spirit and the spirit of his kingdom. The glad words would come to their minds and lips, "Rejoice greatly, O daughter of Zion; shout, O daughter of Jerusalem: behold, thy King cometh unto thee: he is just, and having salvation; lowly, and riding upon an ass, and upon a colt the foal of an ass" (Zech. 9:9).

But Jesus did not have a donkey. So complete had been his self-denial that he did not even have a place to lay his head. But his friends did have such an animal. He knew if he asked for it that they would let him use it; so he sent his disciples to borrow the colt.

It may not seem like much just to lend a donkey, but the Lord had need of it. That made the difference. That amplified many times the importance of their willingness to serve him. We never know when a simple gesture of friendship on our part will take on added meaning because of the special need in the life of the person to whom we direct it. A smile may not be just a smile. It may be an instrument of encouragement to a person who is facing an inner struggle. A letter may not be merely a letter. It may be the messenger of new courage and faith to a person who feels the need of a friend. An act of service may not be a mere act of service. It may be the means of advancing a cause toward victory because it came at a time when it was greatly needed.

Washington had ability and character as he developed his Virginia lands, but there came a time when his country had need of the very qualities he possessed, and because he gave them willingly he became the father of his country. It was just a telephone operator's voice, which she used a thousand times a day, but when a flood came roaring down a Pennsylvania valley, the young woman stayed at her post and called home after home, warning its occupants to flee before the water overtook them. Thus, by her ordinary voice she saved the lives of many people, because in a time of great peril the community needed it. The training we get, the study we do, may seem at the time a waste of effort, but the day may come when we can turn that knowledge and training to great use because the world, or at least our little part of it, has need of it.

The Grace Baptist Church in Philadelphia is one of the great churches in America. As they worshiped in a building known as the Baptist Temple, there was a time when Dr.

Russell H. Conwell, founder of the church and also founder of Temple University, preached to over four thousand persons at the services. The name of Hattie Wyatt is still greatly revered by the members of this congregation. One day, before there was the great building at Broad and Berks Streets, little Hattie Wyatt started to Sunday school in the old building a block behind the present structure. But when she got there, they could not let her in. The building was so crowded on that particular Sunday they could not admit all the children who wanted to get in.

Hattie Wyatt went home greatly disappointed. She began to save her pennies to build a new church building large enough to hold everyone who wanted to come. She saved until she had a total of fifty-seven cents. Hattie Wyatt became ill. She did not get better. One day, after she had gone to heaven, her grieving mother took the fifty-seven cents to Dr. Conwell and told him of her little daughter's project. Deeply moved, the great man told the story to his congregation the following Sunday.

Fifty-seven cents! What can one do with fifty-seven cents when it takes many thousands of dollars to build a building like the Baptist Temple? *But the Lord had need of it.* That fifty-seven cents was to become the spark that set off a movement that resulted in the great church building that was called, at the time it was built, "Conwell's folly," until he demonstrated its need by preaching to a full church Sunday after Sunday.

The Lord hath need of it. It may be a song we can sing, a lesson we can teach, a service we can render. But that song may touch some person's heart, that lesson may set some person's feet on the right path, that service may help to ease the burden on someone's aching shoulders. We may not do anything spectacular. To many our work may go unnoticed. But the Lord has need of your life and mine. He has plans we do not know. We may be the means of influencing someone who will make a large contribution to life. If we are willing to place our lives and talents at his disposal, in his great providence even our lives may make a difference in a time like this.

8

On Knowing
What to Take Seriously

MATTHEW 22:5

WHEN WILLIAM H. DANFORTH, later to become president of the Ralston Purina Company and also founder of the Danforth Foundation, was a child, he did not possess the vigorous health a boy his age should have had. Inclined to be underweight, full of what the people of his area called "swamp poisons," he lacked the physical vitality he needed to grow to strong and sturdy manhood. One day one of his teachers, a good-health enthusiast, challenged him to build a strong body. "I dare you," he said to young Danforth, "to become the healthiest boy in the class." William Danforth might have taken this challenge lightly, but he didn't. He accepted the dare. Launching out on a program of athletics and outdoor activities, he managed to achieve the strong and robust health that stood him in such good stead when he became one of America's outstanding businessmen.

Knowing what to take seriously and what to take lightly is one of life's greatest attributes. As the author of Ecclesiastes might have put it, "There is a time to be serious, and a time to take things lightly," and it is a wise man who knows how to distinguish between the two. Sometimes we get the two reversed. For example, we tend to take injuries to our pride seriously when we should take them lightly and to take lightly a physical ailment or a personal fault that we should take seriously. Sometimes we tend to take lightly the responsibilities and warnings we should take seriously.

Think, for example, of the tragedies that result when people take their marriage vows lightly. Life is strewn with wrecked hopes and lives because at the marriage altar people made promises they evidently did not intend to keep. On the international level we have discovered that there are some things we cannot take lightly we once thought we could. We can no longer take the Communist threat lightly, either at the military or propaganda level. Certainly, we have discovered we can no longer take lightly the Russian boasts of scientific progress. This business of knowing what to take seriously and what to take lightly is one of the most important matters of life.

The tendency to treat lightly what we should take seriously is illustrated in one of Jesus' incomparable stories. A king, he said, arranged for the marriage of his son and sent out his servants to invite the people to the wedding, but they did not come. At the last minute he sent out other servants urging the people to come, telling them about the celebration that had been arranged to follow the ceremony. But Jesus' comment in Matthew 22:5 is, "But they made light of it." In the face of a tremendous opportunity to experience joy and fellowship in the presence of the king, "they made light of it."

One of the points where frequently we find ourselves at odds with Jesus is at the point of what he took seriously and we take lightly. Take the matter of dress and physical security, for example. We attach tremendous importance to these. He took them rather lightly. He said: "Take no thought for your life, what ye shall eat, or what ye shall drink; nor yet for your body, what ye shall put on. Is not the life more than meat, and the body than raiment?" These words sound strange in our material-minded world. He went on to say: "Behold the fowls of the air: for they sow not, neither do they reap, nor gather into barns; yet your heavenly Father feedeth them. . . . Shall he not much more clothe you, O ye of little faith?" He ended up by saying what he took most seriously of all, "Seek ye first the kingdom of God, and his righteousness; and all these things shall be added unto you" (Matt. 6:25, 26–30,33).

Of course, we live in a different culture, and Jesus was not advocating shoddiness. There is no virtue in being shoddy when we can and should be properly dressed. Dr. Ralph Sockman is one of the foremost preachers of our day. His dress, as well as his speech, is always impeccable. A wife whose minister husband was inclined to be careless in his appearance one day said to him, "Dear, why don't you get your suit pressed and your shoes shined, and for once in your life look like Ralph Sockman?"

But people by the thousands do not listen to Dr. Sockman's radio ministry because he is well dressed, but because he is a great minister of Jesus Christ. Dress is important. Physical security is important. He who neglects these things for himself and his family is taking lightly what he should take seriously. But they are not the supremely important thing. What shall it profit a man if he dresses in the latest fashion but has a shoddy soul? Or what shall it profit him if he gains physical security, but neglects his family, his friends, or his spiritual welfare?

Let us look at some of the places where we tend to get our sense of values turned around. For example, sometimes we tend to take our critics lightly and our compliments seriously. As someone has put it, there is nothing wrong with flattery so long as one does not swallow it. We all like a certain measure of it. It helps to give us more self-confidence. But some people seem to live for it. If one received too much flattery, he might get to the place where he longed for it—even felt he deserved it. He might try to trim his sails so as to win men's approval rather than God's. A man went to a dinner where the hostess served hot soup. It was hotter than he realized it would be, so he spluttered the first spoonful back into his plate. Turning to the hostess, he remarked apologetically, "Some men would have swallowed that." It is easy to swallow the nice things that are said about us.

But while we believe our compliments, sometimes we take our criticisms too lightly. We are apt to shrug them off and say, "They are based on ignorance or prejudice." They may be, but we must not ignore them altogether. If a person tries to do what he thinks is right in the sight of the Lord, he is almost bound to get some criticism, but he does not have to care—not if he thinks he has the Lord's approval. But, on the other hand, he had better listen to his critics. It may be God's way of holding up a mirror so he can see himself as others see him.

Or, again, sometimes we take our own selfish ambitions so very seriously and the needs of others much too lightly. Marie Antoinette is one of the tragic figures of history. Every decision was made for her when she was a child, even the decision of whom she would marry. It is understandable, therefore, that, when at an early age she became Queen of France, she let herself go and enjoyed to the full the gaiety and frivolity of French society life, becoming friendly with people who involved her in some of the intrigues that were rife in France and in Europe at the time. However, when she came to the tragic end of her life, she showed more character and courage than her husband had shown as the Dauphin of

France. When they led Marie Antoinette to the guillotine, it was in part retribution for the attitude of the ruling classes toward the revolting masses—an attitude that she herself had once expressed in a regrettable phrase. When told the people had no bread, she is said to have replied, "Then let them eat cake."

You don't do that in this kind of a world. When the church, as it did in Russia, becomes more preoccupied with the kind of vestments the clergy should wear than with the needs and problems of the people, it is a bad day both for the church and the world. It will be a bad day for America if we ever lose sight of the hunger and the aspirations of the people who are trying to rise to new status in our world. If we do not give them help and encouragement, they will become vulnerable to the false promises of communism.

Or, again, sometimes we take our rights very seriously but our responsibilities rather lightly. I once received a letter asking my help in organizing a clergyman's union so we could band together to assert our rights. I refused on the ground that a minister of the gospel has only one right, and that is to serve God wherever he may lead. Other people may legitimately form labor unions, but surely ministers of religion would lose their right to speak in the name of the Lord if they were to band together to demand their rights.

Recently I talked to a college president. I was scheduled to speak in the chapel service of his college. I asked him: "What do you say to young people today? If you were to make this chapel address, what are some of the things you would want to emphasize?" Without hesitation, he replied: "One thing young people need to be told over and over again is to take their responsibilities more seriously. They are quick to demand their rights, but not so quick to assume any responsibility."

But that problem is not limited to youth. Every community and church has that problem. How glad we should be that we live in a free country, enjoying a freedom of thought and action most people of the world have never known. How glad we should be that we are free to read any newspaper printed anywhere in the world, and that our newspapers are free to print news, and not mere propaganda. How glad we should be that we live in a land where we are free to start a new church wherever and whenever we feel there is a need for one. In Russia one must get permission from the government for the use of a building for worship purposes. So far, in all the city of Moscow, the government has seen fit to grant permission for the use of only one building for Protestant worship.

It is one thing to have freedom, but with freedom there always goes responsibility. We have the responsibility to know what we stand for as citizens of a democracy. We have the responsibility to see that our democracy works with equal opportunity for all. We have the responsibility to be trained and educated so we can match wits with the best in the world and can do a good job representing our way of life. We have the responsibility to do our part. We dare not take our rights seriously and our responsibilities lightly.

Finally, we often tend to take the things of the world seriously and the things of religion much too lightly. The world is full of people who take their cocktail parties and their social engagements very seriously but their church attendance lightly. Many of these people are not opposed to religion. They think religion is a good thing for those who want to indulge in it. They just make light of it. Sometimes they laugh at the people who do take their religion seriously, because it is the only way they know to feel superior to those who are trying to live for the Lord.

If there is anything the Bible makes clear, it is that we dare not take the warnings and judgments of God lightly. "It is a fearful thing," says the author of Hebrews, "to fall into the hands of the living God" (10:31). And Paul could write, "Knowing therefore the terror of the Lord, we persuade men" (2 Cor. 5:11). The prophets of Israel warned the people in no uncertain terms of the consequences of their own idolatry and evil acts. Jesus said, "Whoso shall offend one of these little ones which believe in me, it were better for him that a millstone were hanged about his neck, and that he were drowned in the depth of the sea" (Matt. 18:6). And there is that terrifying phrase that occurs again and again, that for him who rejects God's will in Christ "there shall be weeping and gnashing of teeth." This does not sound like something that can be taken lightly.

Some people believe that since God is love and has all eternity at his disposal his patience will outlast the last resistance of the last soul, and finally everyone will be saved, if not in this life, then in the next. But that does not seem to be what the Bible says. The Bible says, "Whatsoever thou shalt bind on earth shall be bound in heaven: and whatsoever thou shalt loose on earth shall be loosed in heaven" (Matt. 16:19). God gives us a lifetime in which to get in tune with his love and will. He will not intrude on our freedom to make our own choice. But having made the choice, we must live with the consequences of our decision. That is part of the nature of a moral universe. The Bible says—and this is an awful warning—that when we get to the marriage of the Lamb some people are not going to get in, because when they received the invitation they "made light of it."

But the Bible also says, "As many as received him, to them gave he power to become the sons of God" (John 1:12). The invitation is out. It is nailed on Calvary. It lies in the straw of

Bethlehem's manger. It shines from an open tomb. The invitation is, "Come unto me, all ye that labour and are heavy laden, and I will give you rest" (Matt. 11:28). The invitation is delivered by the nail-pierced hands of the Saviour himself. We must not—we dare not—make light of it.

9

The Clarion Call to Be Ready

MATTHEW 25:10

HOW VIVIDLY JESUS could tell a story! And what depths of meaning his stories convey! Ten bridesmaids, he said in one story, were on their way to accompany the bridegroom to his wedding. Like most social engagements in a hot country, it was held at night after the heat of the day had begun to subside; so the girls carried lamps with them. What a pretty picture they must have made as they walked along through the night! One can almost hear their happy laughter as they chatted gaily with each other. But (life does not always run on schedule) when they got to his house, the bridegroom tarried—so long, in fact, that one after another the girls dozed off.

When the cry was raised that the bridegroom was coming, the girls made a distressing discovery. Their lamps had burned out. They had waited so long that the oil was used up in their lamps. Five of the girls had come prepared for just such an emergency. They each had brought an extra cruse of oil with them. The other five had made no such preparation. Naturally, the five who had no oil asked the other five to share with them, but these girls pointed out they

64

had just enough oil for themselves. If they shared their oil, none of the girls would have enough left to accompany the bridegroom all the way to the wedding. There was nothing for the five to do but to find their way through the dark to an oil merchant to buy some oil. This they did, but by the time they reached their destination the wedding had already started, the door was closed, and they were not permitted to enter.

How true to life this story is! Life does not always run according to our schedule. Some things are not to be had merely for the asking. Character, moral fiber, skill—these are things which, if one does not have them, must be purchased at the price of dedication and discipline. Some doors do get shut, never to be opened again. But the real punch line of the story—the reason for which the story was told—is found at the very end. "And they that were ready went in with him to the marriage."

"And they that were ready went in . . ." What doors of opportunity are unentered, some of them never to be confronted again, because we are not ready to enter them. "Be prepared" is one of the soundest bits of advice any person can receive. Wisely do we teach it to our Scouts as their motto. Life has many doors, but some of them we are not ready to enter. Only as we approach them carrying the proper light will they open to our knock.

Some doors, for example, we are ready to enter only when we come carrying the light of knowledge. Over the door of his academy at Athens Plato had inscribed these words, "Let no one enter here who is ignorant of geometry." Unfortunately, that would keep many people out. There are vast areas of understanding the nature of the physical universe I can never enter because of my limited knowledge of mathematics. Joseph Priestley, discoverer of oxygen, always attributed his fortunate discovery to chance. Bernard Jaffe comments, "Chance which, to be sure, favored the mind prepared with the proper tools at the most opportune moment." In other words, Priestley, because of his knowledge of chemistry, was ready to recognize and enter the door of a discovery that would have remained closed to one who did not have his knowledge of science. Education opens wonderful doors of knowledge and opportunity that remain forever closed to those who, through lack of study, are not ready to enter them.

Some doors we are ready to enter only when we come carrying the light of love. The way to another person's heart is such a door. Mr. H. T. Joslyn tells of an experience from his school days. He was making things rather difficult for his teacher. One day she asked him to remain after school. He braced himself for the reprimand, and perhaps the punishment, he expected to receive. To his surprise, the teacher talked to him about what she was trying to accomplish with the class. She told him what she thought he could achieve if he would co-operate. As she talked, her eyes filled with tears, and her voice broke.

Mr. Joslyn considers this to be one of the great turning points in his life. If she had reprimanded him as he deserved, he probably would have gone on being difficult to manage. But he discovered his teacher cared—cared about what happened to the class, cared about what happened to him. This insight opened a new door into his heart, and he went on to become a good student and later an outstanding minister of Jesus Christ.

Sophia Fahs writes:

Though I teach with the skill of teachers, and have not love, I am become a thing of mere display, a discordant note in my school of religion. Though I am an artist in story, music and drama, and though I have the keenest understanding of modern theories regarding democratic processes; though I have all faith so as to overcome the most stubborn obstacles to progress, and have not love, it profiteth me nothing.[5]

This is not to disparage the knowledge of good teaching techniques. It stands to reason that a person who is trained is in a better position to express his love more intelligently than one who is untrained. But without love, all the training in the world is not enough. Some doors open only when we approach them carrying the light of love.

Some doors we are ready to enter only when we come carrying the light of faith. Christian experience is such a door. Acceptance with God does not depend on being able to understand everything we read in the Bible. It does not depend on being able to understand the writings of great Christian thinkers, or many people would not be able to enter. Nor does it depend on our ability to merit God's love. If it did, none of us would be able to enter, for none of us possesses the oil of perfection. The humblest, the most unlearned, the most sinful is able to enter into God's love if he comes carrying the light of penitent faith that shows he is willing to surrender his self-will to God, to be cleansed of his sins, and to enter into fellowship with God and with God's people.

But what are some of the doors a Christian should be able to enter? The New Testament suggests several. For one thing, there is the door of service. To the Romans Paul could say, "So, as much as in me is, I am ready to preach the gospel to you that are at Rome also" (Rom. 1:15). To Titus he wrote, "Put them in mind to be subject to principalities

[5] Sophia L. Fahs, "A Teacher's Ode to Love." Adaptation of 1 Cor. 13.

and powers, to obey magistrates, to be ready to every good work" (Titus 3:1).

Readiness to serve in the Master's cause involves two things. It involves both the willingness and the ability to do so. How tragic when one is willing, but is not able! But the cause of Christ is hampered more by those who are able, but are not willing. A trained mind and willing hands and heart are the important attributes of a Christian. If the willingness is there, one can seek the training. If the training is there, one should be willing to dedicate it to the service of God and man.

Again, a Christian should be ready to enter the door of an intelligent witness to his faith. Peter writes, "Be ready always to give an answer to every man that asketh you a reason of the hope that is in you with meekness and fear" (1 Peter 3:15).

Some girls in Westhampton College once came to see me about a problem. A young girl who was not a Christian had moved into their dormitory. The girls had tried to talk to her about being a Christian. When she asked them what a Christian is expected to believe, the girls were at a loss to know what to tell her. Although they knew in a general way, they had not thought through their Christian convictions far enough to be articulate about them. This, unfortunately, is true of many followers of Jesus Christ. How much we need to heed the injunction of Paul, "Study to shew thyself approved unto God, a workman that needeth not to be ashamed, rightly dividing the word of truth" (2 Tim. 2:15).

Most important of all, however, is the door to eternity. Paul could say to Timothy: "I am now ready to be offered, and the time of my departure is at hand. I have fought a good fight, I have finished my course, I have kept the faith: henceforth there is laid up for me a crown of righteousness, which the Lord, the righteous judge, shall give me at that day" (2 Tim. 4:6–8).

Jesus took readiness to enter this door very seriously. In another story he said: "If the goodman of the house had known what hour the thief would come, he would have watched, and not have suffered his house to be broken through. Be ye therefore ready also: for the Son of man cometh at an hour when ye think not" (Luke 12:39).

Nietzsche was one of the most gifted writers of his day. With his genius he could enter doors of philosophical thought that are closed to people who do not share his knowledge of philosophy. But Nietzsche was not ready to die. With all his brilliance, he rejected faith in God. The woman who nursed him in his last illness said she never wanted to see another unbeliever die, because of the fear and agony and hopelessness with which he faced the end of his life.

On the other hand, an old woman in my church lay on her bed of illness. One day the doctor said to her, "Miss Withers, I think I have found something that will do you good." Miss Withers replied: "Then I won't take it. I don't want something that will do me good. I'm tired. I want to go home." Shortly before her death she was told I was out of town. She said, "Tell him I will see him in heaven and not to be too long about getting there either." I would not trade Miss Withers' faith for all the brilliance of all the Nietzsches in the world. When the Saviour came for her, her lamp of faith was lit; she was ready to go with him into the wedding feast.

As children we used to play a game called hide-and-go-seek. While the other children ran to hide, the person who was "it" closed his eyes, counted by fives up to a hundred, then called out, "Ready or not, shall be caught; I'm coming." One day death will call, "Ready or not, I'm coming"; only it won't be a game. This will be real. It will be too late then to wish things had been different; too late then to wish we had known the Lord. While he is willing to listen to us till our last breath, we dare not wait till then.

Of one thing we can be sure: when we do seek his forgiveness and his love, he is ready to give them. The Old Testament writers believed this. The cross confirms it. Nehemiah wrote, "Thou art a God ready to pardon, gracious and merciful, slow to anger, and of great kindness" (9:17). The psalmist echoed this faith by saying, "For thou, Lord, art good, and ready to forgive; and plenteous in mercy unto all them that call upon thee" (86:5). It has been said that one cannot look at the cross and that sublime moment when Jesus prays for his enemies from it without realizing that the God who was in that life and in that moment has an inexhaustible well of forgiveness in his heart.

The door of his promise is there. Now is the time to make sure our lamp is filled with faith. Now is the time to surrender to his love. Now is the time to answer his call. There will be the joyous fellowship of walking the way with him. And when he turns to call us home, whether it be today or whether he tarries, we will be numbered with those of whom it was said, "And they that were ready went in with him to the marriage."

10

Peals of Thunder
or Songs of Angels?

JOHN 12:20–32

IN FACING ANY PROBLEM there are always two things to keep in mind: one is the fact, or facts, with which we are confronted, insofar as it is possible to know them; the other is our interpretation of the facts. The facts themselves we may or may not be able to change, but the interpretation of the facts is pretty largely up to us.

The same thing can happen to two different people and their reaction be as different as day is from night. A symphony concert can put one person to sleep and fill another person with emotions of rapture. The difference is in the persons, not the music. Sorrow can deepen one person's sense of dependence on God and make another person bitter and resentful. Success can make one person grow and another person swell. We live in two worlds at the same time—the world as it is, and the world as we imagine, or interpret, it to be. And so far as our personal happiness is concerned, the second is apt to be the more important of the two.

This difference in the interpretation of the facts we confront is illustrated by an incident that happened in the life of Jesus. Certain Greeks had come to see him. What they said to him we do not know. It has been conjectured they may have invited him to come and teach in their own country, which would have provided him with an opportunity to escape, temporarily at least, from the rising tide of opposition to him from the Jewish leaders.

Whether this is true, and it is only a guess, Jesus did share with the Greeks his philosophy of life and applied it to his own experience. He said, "Except a corn of wheat fall into the ground and die, it abideth alone: but if it die, it bringeth forth much fruit." Then he shared the burden that was in his soul. "Now is my soul troubled; and what shall I say? Father, save me from this hour." "But," he went on to explain, "for this cause came I unto this hour." Then he expressed his personal commitment by saying, "Father, glorify thy name."

When he had spoken, something happened. What it was the people who heard it were never fully agreed on. John says it was a voice from heaven saying, "I have both glorified it, and will glorify it again." But the people did not discern this. Some said it thundered; others said, "An angel spake to him"—one fact, but two widely differing interpretations of the fact. To some it was merely thunder, the presage of a storm. To others, perhaps sensing something of the significance of Jesus' statement, it was an angel's voice expressing heaven's approval of the commitment Jesus had just expressed.

Here you have the two basic interpretations of life—the material and the spiritual, thunder and an angel's voice. Materialism reduces all life to the reverberations of nature. The spiritual interpretation of life does not deny the physical—how could it?—but says, "The earth is the Lord's, and the fulness thereof" (Psalm 24:1). Man is not just an animal but a spiritual being who is capable of communion with God. Materialism reduces life to impersonal atoms dancing around in space. The spiritual interpretation of life says that such things as faith, love, truth, and goodness cannot be explained by a mere collocation of atoms.

Materialism reduces history to one big economic struggle. The spiritual interpretation of life interprets history as "His story" and sees God's hand at the helm of history. Nations may rise and fall, but his truth abides forever. Materialism says man is at the mercy of the flesh. When the body dies, the whole person dies. The spiritual interpretation of life says, "Then shall the dust return to the earth as it was: and the spirit shall return unto God who gave it" (Eccl. 12:7); and "As we have borne the image of the earthy, we shall also bear the image of the heavenly" (1 Cor. 15:49).

The materialist looks at stars and sees nothing more than heavenly objects. The religious man looks at stars and says, "The heavens declare the glory of God; and the firmament sheweth his handywork" (Psalm 19:1). The materialist looks at the body and sees a physical organism with five senses. The religious person looks at the body and says, "Know ye not that your body is the temple of the Holy Ghost which is in you?" (1 Cor. 6:19). The materialist looks at prayer and calls it autosuggestion. The religious person prays and communes with God.

This whole problem is highlighted in our day by the growth of communism. For communism professes to believe in no God. Therefore, it bows to the state as its god and makes Lenin its Messiah. Man becomes a mere tool of the state, since communism does not believe that man is a child of God. Millions of people in the world today are being taught that there is no God, no life after death, no power in prayer. Life is just an economic struggle; therefore love is a weakness. One must learn to hate all his competitors.

For most people outside communism, and for some within,

the distinction is not as clear cut as this. There are gradations of faith. Some people believe in God but never think of him. So far as their living is concerned, they might just as well be thorough-going materialists, for although they profess to believe in God, they live as if there were no God. Others believe in God but never turn to him except in times of trouble. Then there are those who not only believe in God but walk in daily, and even hourly, fellowship with him. They are the ones for whom religion is not a burden but a source of strength that enables them better to carry all other burdens. They are the ones for whom faith in God is not an escape from life but a weapon for the battle.

But what determines how we interpret our experiences and the facts we confront? One obvious answer is our background and training. How we think about certain things, even the kinds of food we like, is often determined by the section of the country or world in which we have lived. The kind of homes in which we have lived, the kind of schools we have attended, the books we have read, the friends with whom we have associated, the groups to which we have belonged, even our age, all help to determine our attitudes toward life—all of which should help us to be a little more tolerant and patient with those with whom we disagree. Given their background, we might more nearly represent their point of view.

But the greatest single factor in determining how we interpret the experiences of life is our faith—what we believe to be eternally true about the nature of the universe in which we live. It makes all the difference in the world whether we believe that this is God's world or man's, whether we believe life is limited to an earthly span or is eternal. On the basis that this is man's world, we might be tempted to say, "Let us eat, drink, and be merry, for tomorrow we die." On the other basis, we know it is imperative to get in tune with God, so he will not have to reject us but can fit us into the symphony of eternity.

The Christian, according to Britisher Donald Hankey, is a person who "bets his life on God," especially as God has revealed himself in Christ, and who hears, in response, angel voices speaking comfort and peace to him out of his joys and sorrows. Without God the path of life leads to fatalism and despair. With God the path of life leads to faith and victory. "The path of the just is as the shining light, that shineth more and more unto the perfect day. The way of the wicked is as darkness: they know not at what they stumble" (Prov. 4:18–19).

The way of faith in God leads to victory over sin. The basic problem in the world today is not missiles, but men. We cannot make a better world until we first get better people. Sin is still man's greatest enemy, an enemy he cannot defeat by himself. And his greatest sin is to act as if he were God, to try to elbow God out of his life so he can live according to the dictates of self-will. As Dr. Reinhold Niebuhr indicates, man's chief problem is not his finiteness, but his sin; but his chief sin is his unwillingness to admit his finiteness. But this, as history both sacred and secular has shown, leads downhill. Only as man learns to confess his sins and seeks God's will is he led out of the Slough of Despond of his own nature into the glorious sunlight of God's love.

The way of faith in God leads to victory over suffering. No normal person likes to suffer, but when suffering comes the important thing is how we deal with it. Do we hear only the reverberations of discomfort, presaging a storm of pain, enforced idleness, and doctor's bills? Or can we, as one person did, even there hear an angel's voice whispering God's truth to our life? For Alice Hansche Mortenson has written:

I needed the quiet, so he drew me aside
Into the shadows where we could confide;
Away from the bustle where all the day long
I hurried and worried when active and strong.
I needed the quiet, though at first I rebelled,
But gently, so gently, my cross he upheld,
And whispered so sweetly of spiritual things,
Though weakened in body, my spirit took wings
To heights never dreamed of when active and gay,
He loved me so gently, He drew me away.
I needed the quiet. No prison my bed,
But a beautiful valley of blessing instead:
A place to grow richer, in Jesus to hide,
I needed the quiet, so he drew me aside.[6]

The way of faith in God leads to victory over death. If ever life seemed to be reduced to the thunder of an ill-deserved fate, it was at Calvary. We are told the heavens themselves literally darkened in that hour. Yet never has God's voice spoken more clearly than it did from the cross. And when Easter came, men knew that what they had thought was the thunder of defeat was an angel's voice through which God was glorifying his cause in the world.

Life has its facts, some of them unpleasant, but Christ has shown us how to deal with them. Have faith in God, and life becomes a place of service and stewardship, not a blind struggle for material ends. Have faith in God, and man becomes our brother to love, not a creature to exploit. Have faith in God, and death becomes a doorway, not a dead-end street. There are times when we, too, will be tempted to say: "Now is my soul troubled; and what shall I say? Father, save me from this hour." But if, like Jesus, we will say in faith, "Father, glorify thy name," heaven will respond, and we will hear an angel's voice speaking peace and joy to our hearts.

---

[6] Alice H. Mortenson, "I Needed the Quiet" (Copyright 1944). Used by permission.

11

The Greatest Miracle of All

JOHN 14:12

A ROMAN CATHOLIC wrote that the weakness of Protestant-ism is revealed by the fact that in all the years of their exist-ence the Protestant churches have not produced a single saint. Of course, everything depends on what one means by the word "saint." Non-Roman churches have produced many thousands of persons every bit as saintly as many of those who have been declared to be saints by the Roman Church. Protestant churches do not canonize their saints, nor are all of them dead.

Let us assume, with the Roman Church, that one must have been associated with some miracle to qualify for sainthood. Every Christian who is faithful to his Lord by helping to sup-port the ministry of some local church is participating in a miracle that, in some ways, is more stupendous than any Jesus performed when he was here in the flesh. What is more, Jesus said that this is what would take place. For Jesus said, "He that believeth on me, the works that I do shall he do also; and greater works than these shall he do; because I go unto my Father" (John 14:12).

If there is any statement in the Bible that is hard to believe, surely this is it. Greater works than Jesus did? How can this ever be? Greater works than he who turned water into wine?

Greater works than he who fed the multitude with a boy's lunch? Greater works than he who stilled the storm? Greater works than he who healed the sick and opened the eyes of the blind? Greater works than he who rose from the dead? On the face of it, this is an impossible statement to believe. And yet Jesus said it. The amazing thing is that it is being fulfilled before our very eyes.

How can this be true? Jesus sometimes spoke to audiences of several thousands. By means of radio it is now possible for a minister like Dr. Ralph Sockman to preach to more people on a single coast-to-coast hookup than Jesus was able to address in his entire ministry. Jesus probably never traveled more than two hundred miles from the place where he was born. By means of aviation it is now possible for a person like Billy Graham to fly more than a hundred thousand miles to proclaim the gospel. And yet this, as wonderful as it is, is hardly what Jesus meant. What, then, did he mean? Surely what he meant was this: "I can only do so much as long as I am in the flesh, but he that believeth in me, the works that I do shall he do also; and greater works than these shall he do—through my new body, the church—because I go to my Father."

Consider how this is true. Once Jesus and the disciples were so lacking in funds that they did not have enough money to pay the Temple tax. Jesus sent the disciples fishing to get the money. But now, by the voluntary gifts of Christians all over the world, churches are able to raise millions of dollars every year for the Christian cause. Many millions of persons give money with no other coercion than their own sense of stewardship and their desire to see the kingdom of God advanced. This itself is a miracle of faith and unselfishness. Much of this money is given to carry the message and ministry of Christ to people in foreign lands whose names, languages, and customs the givers do not know. Here is a miracle of love and faith that transcends national and racial barriers as it seeks to bring all men into the kingdom of one Lord.

In fact, the church itself is a miracle. It is made up of the rich and poor, the young and the old, the learned and the illiterate, the conservative and the liberal. Its members come from every race and nation, representing every kind of opinion, but all are drawn into one sense of fellowship through an experience of God's grace made possible through faith in Christ. Do we begin to see what Jesus must have had in mind when he said, "And greater works than these shall ye do; because I go to my Father"?

We can go on. During his earthly ministry Jesus "had not where to lay his head." But today the church that is his body in the world has built churches, schools, hospitals, orphanages, homes for the aged, retreat centers, denominational programs and headquarters, printing presses, mission stations, and other agencies of witnessing and service, and has done it all for the purpose of sharing the glad news of God's love in Christ. Once Jesus sent seventy of his followers "into every city and place, whither he himself would come" (Luke 10:1). Today churches send thousands of missionaries into almost every country of the world to preach, teach, and heal in Christ's name.

Today, in hospitals built and run by various branches of the Christian church, Christians help to heal more bodies every year than Jesus could possibly touch when he was on earth. Through Christian schools, they teach more children than he could possibly reach when he taught in Galilee. So far as we know, Jesus wrote nothing except once to make some markings in the dust with his finger. Today scores of religious publishing houses print tens of thousands of Bibles, books, tracts, lesson helps, and other printed materials to help proclaim and interpret the Christian message. Do we begin to see what Jesus must have meant when he said, "And greater works than these shall ye do; because I go to my Father"?

Perhaps most people do not think of their participation in the life of the church in this way. They do not think that because they add their gifts to the contributions millions of other Christians are making, because they add their service to the service of hundreds of thousands of other Christian workers, their witness to the witness of all other faithful Christians, their prayers to the millions of prayers that ascend daily to the Father, their love and influence to the love and influence of Christians around the world, they are helping to accomplish the miracle of the greatest volume of outpoured love and service this world has ever seen—a love and service that ask nothing in return save that others have the opportunity to know the joy and hope of knowing and serving Christ.

Who would want to be left out of such a glorious enterprise? Yet some person may be tempted to think that since he is only one Christian in several millions, since his contribution is such an infinitesimal part of what Christians around the world are able to give and do, it makes little difference whether he does his part or not. Of course, if everyone thought this way, there would be no church.

In the front of the Delaware Avenue Baptist Church in Buffalo, New York, there is a lovely mosaic of angels arching over the baptistry. Suppose one piece of that mosaic were to fall out of the eye of one of the angels; which would the members of the congregation be most apt to notice—the many pieces that remained in place, or the spot where one had fallen out? Suppose one key of a piano did not play;

which would a concert artist notice most—the eighty-seven remaining keys that did play, or the one that did not? Suppose someone had a front tooth missing; which would friends notice most when he smiled—the thirty-one remaining teeth, or the hole where one was missing?

Susanna Wesley, the mother of John and Charles Wesley, had seventeen other children in twenty years, but because of the high infant mortality rate of those days she raised only nine of them beyond infancy. Did she shrug off the loss of ten because she had nine left? A part of Susanna Wesley went into every one of those ten graves. They were her children, too. And we are God's children. He is as conscious of his entire family as Susanna Wesley was of hers. Do we think he does not notice if we fail to give him our love or if we fail to do our part?

Oh, of course, volume alone does not produce the miracle. It is not the amount of property the churches own that determines the extent of their influence, but the faith with which they believe and tell their message and express God's love in the world. It is not the volume of prayers that are uttered, but the faith and sincerity with which they are prayed. It is not just the number of Christians in the world, but the extent of their dedication to their faith. It is not their wealth and wisdom, although both of these can be used in the service of the Lord, but the extent to which they let themselves be used as a channel of God's love. It is the inner spirit of self-giving that makes the other important.

For, after all, we do not perform the miracle; God does that. A well-known clergyman once was approached by a reeling drunk man on a busy city street. "You don't know me, do you?" said the drunk man. "Should I?" asked the minister. "You should," replied the drunk man; "I'm one of your converts." The minister eyed the drunk man sadly, then said: "You must be right. You must be one of *my* converts; you don't look like one of the Lord's."

We don't do the healing. God is the Great Physician. But if we help to provide hospitals and send out missionary doctors and nurses, we can help him to heal more bodies today than Jesus could heal in his limited time on earth. We cannot all go as missionaries, but we can help to send those whom God calls into this service. We cannot do the converting; that is the work of the Holy Spirit. But we can tell the story of God's love. If a hundred thousand Christians would speak today of their faith in Christ to a hundred thousand persons who are indifferent to his call, and would do it with conviction and dedication, the miracle of which Jesus spoke could happen all over again. More people would be invited in a single day to follow Christ than all the disciples could reach in their lifetime.

God still speaks to men through his church. The miracle still goes on. Because he has called us not only into his love but to be living cells in his body, which is the church, we, too, can preach the gospel to the poor, heal the brokenhearted, preach deliverance to the captives and recovery of sight to the blind. We, too, can help to set at liberty them that are bruised and preach the acceptable year of the Lord, and we can do it on a scale Jesus and the disciples could never match, because we have with us all the members and resources of Christian churches today. Therefore, by accepting his love and answering his call to serve him through the church, we can claim his amazing promise, "He that believeth on me, the works that I do shall he do also; and greater works than these shall he do; because I go unto my Father."

12

Tensions Good and Bad

JOHN 14:27; MATTHEW 10:34

SEVERAL YEARS AGO a story appeared about a farmer who decided to move into town and employ a hired man to run his farm. In interviewing a man for the job, the farmer asked him if he knew how to plow, how to milk a cow, and so on. Then he asked, "What do you know how to do best?" To this the man replied, "How to sleep on a windy night." This was a surprising answer, but since he was the only man available at the time, the farmer hired him.

Some time later a fierce gale blew up. The owner of the farm, remembering the hired man's words, had visions of the man sleeping while the hay lay uncovered and the cows stood in the field at the mercy of the storm. So he hurried to the farm as fast as he could travel. When he got there, he found the hay under cover, all the cows safe in their stalls, and the hired man asleep in the house. Then he knew what the hired man had meant. He was able to sleep because he had taken care of the chores. If the hay had been uncovered and the cows had been out in the storm, he would not have been able to sleep on a windy night.

Many of us are not able to relax so easily as the hired man. For one thing, even if most of us worked twelve hours a day and took no time out for relaxation, we still would not be able to finish all the work that needs to be done. Always there is more to do, and this often makes us feel a sense of pressure and tension.

Moreover, we live at such a tempo that tension is almost an inevitable result. Our forefathers worked hard and got tired too, but they did not live at the same pace. They could not speed along the highways at sixty or seventy miles an hour, but had to be content with the more leisurely gait of a horse-drawn vehicle. They developed patience waiting for the crops to grow, whereas we rush to the store and get upset if we have to wait in line to pay for our groceries. They took time to worship, to enjoy their neighbors, and to enjoy family fellowship and conversation. We rush about, shout to each other in passing, and if we are ever home, television prevents any serious attempt at conversation. As for worship, we sing, "O rest in the Lord, wait patiently for him," then fidget if the sermon goes over twenty minutes. It is a rare person any more who takes time for serious reflection and meditation. We do not take time to pray. Whether he knew it or not, Joseph Scriven was speaking for our whole age when he wrote, "Oh, what peace we often forfeit, Oh, what needless pain we bear, all because we do not carry ev'rything to God in prayer!"

But our greatest tensions come from within, and the greatest tensions of all come from a sense of guilt. This kind of tension can tear us apart. The psalmist describes this kind of tension by saying, "When I kept silence, my bones waxed old through my roaring all the day long" (Psalm 32:3). So long as he kept silent and refused to confess his sin, even his health suffered as a result of the silent "roaring" of his conscience. Then he says, "I acknowledged my sin unto thee . . . and thou forgavest the iniquity of my sin." Out of a sense of joy and relief he cries, "For this shall every one that is godly pray unto thee in a time when thou mayest be found: surely in the floods of great waters they shall not come nigh unto him" (Psalm 32:5–6). The psalmist is right. "Blessed is he whose transgression is forgiven, whose sin is covered" (Psalm 32:1).

True religion addresses itself to such tensions. To all who need it it offers peace. To the hurried and harried it says, "Cast thy burden upon the Lord, and he shall sustain thee" (Psalm 55:22). To the tired and discouraged it says, "They that wait upon the Lord shall renew their strength; they shall mount up with wings as eagles; they shall run, and not be weary; and they shall walk, and not faint" (Isa. 40:31). To the sinful it says, "If we confess our sins, he is faithful and just to forgive us our sins, and to cleanse us from all unrighteousness" (1 John 1:9). It has a solution for all the problems of life.

But there is another side to the picture. Faith in God destroys tensions; it also creates them. It both gives us peace of mind and takes it away. It gives us inward peace, but throws us into conflict with a sinful world. The same Christ who said, "My peace I give unto you" (John 14:27), also said, "I came not to send peace, but a sword" (Matt. 10:34). If we are truly Christian, we not only enjoy the peace of a surrendered will, we cry out with Jesus to a sinful world, "If thou hadst known, even thou . . . the things which belong unto thy peace!" (Luke 19:42). How can one be relaxed in the face of the world's sin and need? How can one be a Christian whose love and concern for mankind do not lead him to cry out in protest against the forces of evil that seek to engulf men's lives and destroy their souls? We have said much in recent times about the need to live an adjusted life. We have forgotten one can become so adjusted to his world he becomes complacent about the evils around him. We have said so much about peace of mind we have forgotten Jesus calls us into conflict with the forces of sin and evil.

For one thing, if a person is sensitive to the will of God, he is bound to feel a sense of tension between what the world says and expects and what God says and expects. The world says through practically every advertisement we see, "Indulge yourself." God says, "Deny yourself." The world says of social evils, "They're controversial; don't mention them." God says, "They're evil; denounce them."

For some people this is no problem, because they do not try to look at life through God's eyes. They have not heard his voice calling them to prophetic vision and utterance. They are content to let the world go its way while they go theirs. They do not challenge the standards of the world. Why be different? If the world says, "Drink," they drink. If the world says, "Keep silent," they keep silent.

But in every age there are those who cannot keep silent. The word of God is in them, and they must speak out against all that violates his will for human lives.

One of the most graphic portrayals of this kind of tension is seen in the experience of Jeremiah. With a heavy heart Jeremiah felt called of God to denounce his country's sins and to declare God's judgment upon Judah. The people did not listen to him. They listened instead to Amaziah, who prophesied the things they wanted to hear. Jeremiah was arrested and placed in stocks near the Temple. The passing throng mocked and derided him. Jeremiah's thoughts churned within him. "O Lord," he cried, "thou hast deceived me, and I was deceived" (Jer. 20:7). How little Jeremiah had guessed what lay in store for him when he answered God's call. "I am in derision daily," he moaned, "every one mocketh me. . . . The word of the Lord was made a reproach unto me, and a derision, daily."

Jeremiah decided he would no longer speak in the name of the Lord. "Then I said, I will not make mention of him, nor speak any more in his name. But . . ." Here was Jeremiah's tension. "But his word was in mine heart as a burning fire shut up in my bones . . . and I could not stay" (Jer. 20:9). In the face of God's message burning in his heart Jeremiah simply could not keep silent.

Frances Willard, founder of the Woman's Christian Temperance Union, knew this kind of tension. She knew the love of a very fine college president who wanted to marry her. But she also knew that if she worked for the cause of temperance she would be unpopular with many, and would become the object of derision and scorn. She refused to marry lest the opposition directed against her would jeopardize the work of the man who loved her. For concerning the evils of the liquor traffic she could not keep silent. God's word was in her heart like a burning fire, and she could not stay her tongue.

Jesus, too, felt this kind of tension—not tension in the sense we so often know it, not the tension of anxiety. One gets the impression as he reads the Gospels that Jesus walked through the most trying situations without the tension caused by resentment and despair. Others might want to call down fire from heaven. He quietly said he came not to destroy but to save (Luke 9:54). Others might be quick to use the sword. He spoke quietly about the resources of heaven (Matt. 26:51–52).

Yet there was the tension of concern over the plight of his people. "Ye know that the princes of the Gentiles exercise dominion over them, and they that are great exercise authority upon them. But it shall not be so among you" (Matt. 20:25–26). There was the tension of heartbreak over their blindness. "O Jerusalem, Jerusalem, thou that killest the prophets, and stonest them which are sent unto thee, how often would I have gathered thy children together, even as a hen gathereth her chickens under her wings, and ye would not!" (Matt. 23:37). There was the tension of indignation over the exploitation of the poor and the desecration of the Temple. "It is written, My house shall be called the house of prayer; but ye have made it a den of thieves" (Matt. 21:13). Others might suffer such practices in silence, but not Jesus—not when they took unfair advantage of innocent people and defamed the worship of God. It was not safe to speak out against them, but how could he keep silent when the people were not safe from the unscrupulous practices of greedy and dishonest men?

There was also the tension between the hard way of the cross and the desire to find some other way to fulfil God's will. Why should it surprise us that Jesus experienced such tension? If he was to be tempted in all points like as we are, he had to face even this temptation to draw back from the cruel consequences he would suffer as a result of his stand. To the Greeks who sought him he said, "Now is my soul troubled; and what shall I say? Father, save me from this hour: but," he went on, "for this cause came I unto this hour" (John 12:27). Here was his tension—whether to face the necessity of the cross or to try to find some other way.

That it was no easy problem to resolve is indicated by his agony in the garden of Gethsemane, where "being in an agony he prayed more earnestly: and his sweat was as it were great drops of blood falling down to the ground" (Luke 22:44). This was no play acting. This was a struggle in which he was wrestling "not against flesh and blood, but against principalities, against powers, against the rulers of the darkness of this world, against spiritual wickedness in high places" (Eph. 6:12). And he won. Out of this struggle came the world's most significant and far-reaching decision.

"Nevertheless," he said to the Father, "not as I will, but as thou wilt" (Matt. 26:39).

Still this kind of tension goes on in the hearts of dedicated men and women. There are those, for example, who have experienced this tension in regard to the race problem. It would have been so much easier for them to refrain from mentioning it. The world—and sometimes even the churches —asked only that they keep silent on this issue. But they could not remain completely silent. In love and sorrow they felt they must speak some word for better racial attitudes and understanding, and some of them paid for it with their jobs. Like their Master before them, they have wept over their land, and their tears have shone with the iridescence of God's holy will and love.

Or again, if one is sensitive to God's will for his life, he is bound to experience tension between what he is and what he knows God wants him to be.

This, also, is not a problem with many. They do not listen to the voice of God. They do not see the need to change. They do not live with the image of Christ in their mind, and so they are satisfied with themselves as they are.

The Pharisee who went up to the Temple to pray was such a man. If ever a man advertised his complete satisfaction with himself, surely it was he. He spent his entire time giving God a list of particulars about his goodness. "God," he said, "I thank thee, that I am not as other men are, extortioners, unjust, adulterers, or even as this publican. I fast twice in the week, I give tithes of all that I possess" (Luke 18:11–12). Thus he advertised his complete satisfaction with himself as he was. He failed to sense his lack of concern for others. He failed to sense his need for God. He failed to see that while he may have been better than the publican, he was a long sea mile from being what God wanted him to be. If he had stopped comparing himself with the publican and had begun to compare himself with Jesus, he would have realized how little and sinful and self contained he really was. He was right; he was not like the publican. He was so full of complacency and self-satisfaction that, for all his gifts, God could not use him, whereas the publican was so conscious of his faults, so desirous of receiving God's help and forgiveness that, in spite of his sins and shortcomings, God could begin to use him.

But it is the very tension set up by the call of God that calls forth some of life's highest and noblest living. It is not they who ignore the world's needs who are its greatest benefactors, but they who cannot rest until they have done something to respond to that need. It is not they who ignore God's call who experience the greatest satisfaction and peace, but they who say, "Here am I, Lord, send me." A violin, no matter how carefully made or skilfully played, cannot bring forth music unless its strings are under tension. A watch, even though it had the finest Swiss movement made, could not keep time unless its mainspring was under tension. And a Christian who feels no tension between what he knows himself and the world to be and what he knows is right can never feel the vibrations of God's grace or enable the world to see it is time to repent.

Out of such tension—dissatisfaction with self and the world, confidence and faith in God's goodness and love— God can produce the melody of a great witness to his truth and righteousness. It is Jeremiah, not Amaziah, whose life sings today. Out of the tension of Jeremiah's faith and concern there was produced a great message that still lives to enlighten and challenge the world. Out of Frances Willard's tension of concern and indignation there grew a great temperance movement that once swept this nation like a tidal wave, and the memory of her courage and dedication continues to inspire thousands who still believe in the cause for which she lived. Surely the cross is the acme of all tension caused by answering God's call. There one's body hung stretched between heaven and earth. But because Jesus was willing to go even that far, because he was "obedient unto death, even the death of the cross" (Phil. 2:8), God has used that obedience and sacrifice to sing the song of man's greatest hope. Because Jesus accepted the tensions of Calvary, there has vibrated through two thousand years of history and around the world the glorious song of God's redemptive love.

The paradox is evident. The Christian faith gives us inner peace. It also flings us into conflict with the forces of injustice and evil in the world. It sometimes makes us take a stand that is both unpopular and dangerous. But out of the very tensions aroused by such a stand there sounds the song of hope and deliverance for those who are the victims of life's evil forces. If we accept the peace of God's love, we must also grasp the sword of his wrath and go forth to do battle with sin, that others may come to know the peace that passeth understanding.

13

Loving Promises
for Lonely People

JOHN 15:15; 16:7

IT WAS NEAR THE END of Jesus' earthly ministry. Pretty soon the disciples would be left to face a hostile world alone. At times they would be discouraged. At times they would be lonely. Anticipating these days, Jesus speaks to them wonderful words of comfort and assurance. "Henceforth," he says, "I call you not servants; for the servant knoweth not what his lord doeth: but I have called you friends; for all things that I have heard of my Father I have made known unto you." And again, "If I go not away, the Comforter will not come unto you; but if I depart, I will send him unto you."

Loneliness can be a desperate experience. Several years ago Admiral Richard E. Byrd went to Little America to make scientific observations of that polar region. For six months he lived absolutely alone in a station that had been built for that purpose. During that time he saw no other face, he heard no other voice except by short wave radio. Upon returning home, he wrote a vivid account of his isolated vigil at the South Pole under the simple title *Alone*.

Not many people experience such a prolonged period of solitude. Millions, however, and at times all of us, experience some degree of loneliness. For loneliness for many people is one of the major problems with which they have to contend. This is especially true in large cities where people "touch elbows with thousands, but hearts with few." A widely read book, *The Lonely Crowd* by David Riesman and others, focuses attention on the terrible loneliness at the heart of our great American cities. While Admiral Byrd was alone, he did have the stimulus of his scientific observations, and although at times his voluntary loneliness must have been an ordeal, he knew that at the end of six months his vigil would be over. There are millions, however, particularly in our large cities, for whom the experience of loneliness is a never-ending prospect.

There is loneliness everywhere. There is the loneliness of those who, deprived of family life, live by themselves. There is the loneliness of missionaries far from loved ones. There is the loneliness of young people away from home—some in military service, some in college, some starting out on their own. Here is a girl, and her name is legion, living alone in a large city, who, in order to escape her loneliness, accepts the lower standards of those who do not share her ideals. Here is a woman calling a pastor to say: "My husband and I keep up the pretenses of family life, but he doesn't love me any more. I might just as well be a servant in the house. Would I not be justified, even though I am a married woman, in going out with other men who would help me forget my loneliness?"

Here is a child who feels unwanted by his family, and this feeling leaves him with psychological scars all the rest of his life. Here is a child who feels rejected by the society in which he lives. He wants all the nice things he thinks all the other people have—the lovely things he sees advertised in newspapers and displayed in store windows; so he steals in order to get them.

There is the loneliness of the sickroom, where day after day, and sometimes week after week, and even year after year, someone stares at the same four walls and ceiling, able to see only the people who come to see him. There is the loneliness of the bereaved, separated from a loved one whose companionship has meant everything across the years. There is the loneliness of the aged, feeling unwanted and in the way. There is the loneliness of the great, living life in a fish bowl, knowing their every move and utterance is under public scrutiny. How often they must pine for a more normal existence in which they would be freer to enjoy the companionship of family and friends. Yes, loneliness is one of the real problems of life for millions of people.

Jesus experienced this problem of loneliness. He knew about it right in his own home. One of the tragedies of his earthly life was that his own brothers, and at times even his own mother, did not understand him, and his brothers were unsympathetic to his cause. It took Jesus' resurrection to convince James and Jude that what Jesus had said was true. As John so strikingly puts it, "He came unto his own, and his own received him not" (1:11). There is real pathos in Jesus' words, "A prophet is not without honour, but in his own country, and among his own kin, and in his own house" (Mark 6:4).

Jesus knew the loneliness of the wilderness where he was "forty days tempted of the devil." He knew the loneliness of being deserted. Anyone who takes a stand for a great principle is bound to know loneliness, for he will discover to his dismay that sometimes the very people on whom he thought he could count the most do not understand him or will not stand by him. What sadness there must have been in Jesus' voice when he asked the disciples, "Will you also go away?"

There was the deep loneliness of Gethsemane. If ever he

wanted someone to stand by him, he wanted it then. He took with him the three men on whom he thought he could most depend. But they were human, and they were tired; and they fell asleep. Jesus had to say, "Could ye not watch with me one hour?"

And there was the awful loneliness of the cross, when for a moment it seemed as if God himself had deserted him. All the agony of all the lonely hearts in the world is caught up in that cry, "My God, my God, why hast thou forsaken me?" Sometimes we, too, know the loneliness and agony of saying, "My God, why?"

Loneliness is an old problem. One of the first things to be said about it is that there are times when we need to be alone. Every person needs some time to be alone to think and pray. Jesus knew that. How often he sought the solitude of the hills for meditation and prayer. He said, "When thou prayest, enter into thy closet, and when thou hast shut thy door, pray to thy Father which is in secret; and thy Father which seeth in secret shall reward thee openly" (Matt. 6:6).

This is part of our problem. We are so busy, and so much a part of the world of people, we have little time or chance to be alone. I know a man who quite regularly drives his car out of town, parks by a bridge, and walks along the river. He says it is the only way he can be alone. Even in his home there is the noise of the children, and his phone is constantly ringing, breaking in on his desire for a few moments of quiet. I know another man who sometimes in the midst of a busy day feels the need for a few minutes of quiet and prayer. He leaves his desk, jumps into a taxi, and goes to a nearby church —it is not always the same church—for a half hour alone with his thoughts and his God.

I read the story of a woman who slipped into a church to pray. While she was there, a well-dressed man entered the church and walked up to the altar. There he knelt and placed his hands on the altar as he prayed. When he left the church, he held his hands out in front of him as if loath to touch anything after having consecrated them at the altar. The next day the woman read that a famous surgeon in the city had performed a very delicate brain operation, and she always believed that the famous surgeon and the man at the altar were one.

The next thing we would want to say about this problem is that each of us should be the kind of person who is fit to be with when he is alone. Perhaps the best-known poem of Edgar Guest is the one entitled "Myself," in which he says:

> I have to live with myself, and so
> I want to be fit for myself to know.

Children are so refreshing. A little girl was talking to herself while she played. An adult asked her why she was talking to herself, and without any show of conceit she replied, "Because I'm nice to talk to." It is nice to be nice to talk to when one has to be alone.

But while we all need some time to be alone, and while each of us should be the kind of person who can make the most of periods of solitude, we are so made that we do need friendship and are desperately unhappy without it. Paul is coming up the Appian highway. If ever a man had a reason to be discouraged, surely it was he. He was no longer a young man. He had suffered cruelly for his faith. He had just been shipwrecked. He was being taken as a prisoner to Rome to face trial on a trumped-up charge. Then Paul and his party saw a group of people coming forward to meet them. They were Christians from Rome, "whom when Paul saw," Luke tells us, "he thanked God, and took courage" (Acts 28:15).

If we are not lonely, we can thank God for the loved ones and friends who give us love and courage. Some people make friends more easily than others. The author of Proverbs says, "A man that hath friends must shew himself friendly" (18:24). It is almost a law of life that a smile tends to beget a smile, a frown a frown. People treat us the way we treat them. We tend to treat them the way they treat us.

Again children are so wonderful at this point. They are so unself-conscious in the freedom with which they make friends. We had not been in our parsonage an hour till a little girl was at our door to see if we had any little girls with whom she could play. Children can find out in one hour what it would take their parents months to learn about a neighborhood. Here is a little boy knocking at our door to ask, "Did you mean for Dick to give me this?" No, I did not mean for Dick to give him that. That was a new telephoto lens for my camera that had been given to me by my church. Dick did not know his father could not have afforded to buy it for himself. All he knew was that he had made a new friend.

The trouble is that we live in a world where it is not always safe to trust other people. What a tragedy that is! It hurts me to pass someone along the road who needs a lift, yet I have been warned so often of the danger of giving a ride to someone who may presume on the kindness to commit a crime. That is why the Christian basis for friendship is so important. I was in Japan shortly after World War II. I was of a different race. I could not speak their language. Our nations had just been at war with each other. But I was a Christian, so my fellow Christians there made me welcome.

During the war a little London boy was separated from his parents. He could not even remember his name. When asked by a worker who he was, he replied through his sobs, "I ain't nobody's nothin'." How many people in the world feel as rejected and disconsolate. This is part of the mission of the church—to throw its arms around the unloved and unwanted until they feel that in the sight of God and within the Christian fellowship everybody is somebody's something.

For the Bible goes deeper than mere human friendship. The Old Testament says, "There is a friend that sticketh closer than a brother" (Prov. 18:24). The New Testament capitalizes the word "Friend" and presents Jesus as the perfect Friend.

Jesus knew that friendship must go deeper than just the human level. He knew how in his day many by servitude were robbed of a sense of human dignity and worth. So to the disciples he said, "Henceforth I call you not servants . . . but I have called you friends." If, as has been suggested, the basic question of life is "Is the universe friendly?" the Christian answer is a ringing yes. He in whose face has shined "the light of the knowledge of the glory of God" has called us friends. More than that, he has defined God as Friend. Indeed, it was Jesus' friendship that got him into trouble with the leaders of his day, for in the name of the Great Physician he offered his healing friendship to the sick of soul, the social outcast, the publican and sinner.

No wonder we sing "Jesus, Friend of Sinners." No wonder "What a Friend We Have in Jesus" is a favorite hymn of so many. When God walked the earth in the person of Jesus, he came not as a *Führer*, but as Friend. And life, despite its rich friendships, is never fully satisfied until we experience friendship at the deeper level where "deep calleth unto deep" beneath the noise of life's waterspouts; until we gain the confidence that the Christian who lives by faith and prayer is never alone because God is always present.

This is all-important, for there are times when all of us must walk alone. Sometimes we must go down into some valley of decision, where not even a wife or husband can go with us all the way. We must make the decision alone. Sometimes we must go through the valley of suffering and pain alone; no one else can suffer the pain for us. Sometimes our friends may say, "I'd give anything if I could suffer this instead of you." But they cannot. The pain is ours, and we must bear it.

And one day, of course, we will go on the loneliest journey of all—but not alone, for even there in the valley of the shadow of death One will be with us whose rod and staff will comfort us. Dr. Shields Hardin tells of moving into a new development where the street lights had not yet been installed. His little boy was given the responsibility of placing the empty milk bottles on the porch after supper so they would be ready early in the morning for the milkman. One evening the boy went to the door and hesitated. His father asked him why he waited. The boy replied, "It's too dark to go out there tonight without a father." When the father walked out on the porch, the boy did not even think of the darkness. He went out laughing and talking to put the milk bottles in their places.

When we go into the valley of decision, we do not go alone. One is there to guide us. When we walk into the valley of pain, we do not go alone. One who knows all about suffering is there to sustain us. When we walk into the valley of the shadow of death, we need not go alone. One who knows the way has promised to be with us—One who does not call us servant, but friend.

14

The Trial
That Got Reversed

2 Corinthians 5:10

One often hears of a decision of a lower court being reversed by a higher court. Occasionally a court will, for good reason, reverse one of its own former decisions. But this message is about a whole trial that got reversed, so that the prisoner became the judge and the judge stands as one of those on trial.

The trial of Jesus is one of the most shocking incidents in history. As an instrument of justice, it was an utter farce. The accusers of Jesus tried to set themselves up as judge and jury as well and brazenly announced the only sentence for which they would settle. The judge of the trial publicly pronounced that the prisoner was innocent, and then turned around and condemned him to death because he was afraid of someone who wasn't even there.

It is not easy to reconstruct the exact order of the events in the last night and morning of Jesus' life, but by telescoping the various Gospel accounts of the trial of Jesus, one gets a picture something like this. The trial of Jesus divides itself into two halves, the Jewish half and the Roman half, and there seem to be three steps in each half.

100

When Jesus was arrested in the garden of Gethsemane, it seems that he was taken first to the home of Annas, the father-in-law of Caiaphas, the high priest. There were two reasons for this. One was that it would permit Annas, an experienced public figure, to subject Jesus to preliminary questioning in the hope that he would say something that could be used against him at the trial. The second reason was that it would give Caiaphas a chance to rout the members of the Sanhedrin out of their beds to hold a hastily summoned meeting in the middle of the night. This was absolutely illegal since, according to Jewish law, a trial calling for capital punishment could not be held until after sunrise of the day following the arrest of the prisoner. But Caiaphas was desperate. He felt the only way to deal with Jesus was to get rid of him, and now that Jesus was in his hands, he wanted to carry out his plans quickly before the friends of Jesus could be aroused to come to his support.

Annas soon saw he would get nowhere with his questioning; so Jesus was taken to Caiaphas' palace to stand trial before the Sanhedrin. Caiaphas knew that a religious charge would have no weight in a Roman court; so the first charge brought against Jesus was that he threatened to destroy the Temple. False witnesses were called, but they could not agree on what Jesus had said; so the charge fell for lack of corroborating evidence.

Then Caiaphas did the second illegal thing. It was illegal to try the same person on two charges in the same trial; but the first charge having failed, Caiaphas then introduced the charge of blasphemy—that Jesus sought to equate himself with God. Caiaphas asked Jesus the direct question, "I adjure thee by the living God, that thou tell us whether thou be the Christ, the Son of God." Jesus answered, "Thou hast said." Then he added, "I say unto you, Hereafter shall ye see the Son of man sitting on the right hand of power, and coming in the clouds of heaven" (Matt. 26:63–64). This was all Caiaphas needed. In mock remorse he tore his garments and called for the vote. And while the vote was not unanimous (we know that Joseph of Arimathea voted in the negative), the Sanhedrin voted that Jesus was worthy of death. As Jesus was led from the courtroom, he turned and saw Peter, and Peter, who had just denied knowing him, seeing his glance, went out and wept bitterly.

Early in the morning there seems to have been another meeting of the Sanhedrin, not to try Jesus further, but to acquaint the members who had not been reached during the night with what had taken place and to plot further the strategy of Jesus' accusers when they brought their prisoner before Pilate.

It was Passover time; so the accusers of Jesus persuaded Pilate to hold the trial outside his palace so they would not incur ceremonial defilement by entering a Gentile building. The charge brought against Jesus was a vaguely worded accusation, "he stirreth up the people, teaching throughout all Jewry, beginning from Galilee to this place" (Luke 23:5). Pilate suspected the trouble was religious in nature. He was looking for a way out, and mention of Galilee suggested such a way. He reminded them that Herod was the person to try a Galilean, and since Herod was in the city attending the Passover, Pilate sent Jesus to him.

Herod was delighted. He was pleased, in the first place, that Pilate would pay that much attention to him. He was delighted, in the second place, because he hoped to see Jesus perform a miracle. So he asked Jesus to perform a sign to show he was the Son of God. When Jesus met this kind of request with regal silence, Herod showed his childishness by having Jesus mocked before returning him to Pilate.

Faced again with this puzzling problem, Pilate tried three different ways to avoid the decision for which Jesus' accusers were clamoring. He offered to release to them either Jesus or Barabbas, thinking they would choose Jesus, but they chose Barabbas. He thought if he had Jesus whipped it would satisfy the crowd, but it didn't. Finally, he washed his hands in public to signify his desire to avoid responsibility in this case, but he couldn't. He, and only he, had the authority to condemn Jesus to death. Then the accusers of Jesus played their trump card. "If thou let this man go," they cried, "thou art not Caesar's friend: whosoever maketh himself a king speaketh against Caesar" (John 19:12). That did the trick. It would never do to let the rumor get back to Rome that Pilate was being soft in dealing with so-called subversives. So, rather than incur unfavorable publicity in Rome, Pilate turned Jesus over to the soldiers to be crucified.

The same forces that put Jesus on the cross then are in the world today. But there is one sense in which the situation is completely reversed. Paul suggests this complete reversal in 2 Corinthians 5:10 when he says, "For we must all appear before the judgment seat of Christ." It is no longer Jesus who is on trial. Now Caiaphas is on trial, the Sanhedrin is on trial, Pilate is on trial, the mob is on trial, the world is on trial, all are on trial—before Jesus.

For one thing, the world is on trial before the purity of Jesus. Think of the purity of this man. His enemies would have done anything to destroy him. Yet he could ask them, "Which of you convinceth me of sin?" and they were silent, because they could not put their finger on one tiny flaw in his moral character. Of all men who ever lived, it could be said of him alone that tempted in all points as we are, yet he was without sin. It is old-fashioned language, but it speaks the truth:

He's the Lily of the Valley, the Bright and Morning Star,
He's the fairest of ten thousand to my soul.

But when we turn from Jesus to us, the picture is not the same. Purity is not one of the outstanding characteristics of our age—sophistication maybe, so-called realism perhaps, but not purity. Look at today's newsstands, theaters, novels, advertisements, and you get the impression that never since the licentious days of the Roman Empire has sex been so blatantly exploited; but people are not the happier because of it.

Dr. Oscar Blackwelder, who ministered for many years in a church near the Supreme Court building, points out that the marble of which the Supreme Court building is made is so white it fairly blinds one to look at it under the summer sun, but when it snows, the Supreme Court building looks gray. Our whitest whiteness is a dismal gray compared to the purity and perfection of Jesus.

A noted churchman collects and sings old religious folk songs. After hearing him sing some of these lovely songs, a friend suggested that life would have to be simpler and purer to produce such music. He agreed. "One of the reasons," he said, "why I like to collect and sing these old religious songs is that after dealing all day with the muddiness of people's problems, I can come to my room, sing some of these songs, and it is like taking a spiritual bath." The world stands on trial today before the purity of Jesus.

The world stands on trial before the love of Jesus. If he had loved others less and himself more, he might have escaped the cross, but "having loved his own . . . he loved them unto the end" (John 13:1). We love, too, but look at what we love. We love self, prestige, power. We stand on trial before the love of Jesus.

One day Jesus healed a Gadarene demoniac. After hav-

ing sought shelter from the elements by living in the sepul-
chers in the cemetery, and having run naked in his madness
frightening the people so that they tried to chain him, now
the man stood quiet, wrapped in a borrowed garment and
clothed again in his right mind. During this incident some
pigs plunged over a cliff into the sea, and were drowned.
When the people of the village came out to see what was
happening, they saw what had happened to the pigs, and
ignoring what had happened to the man, they begged Jesus
to depart from their coasts. Pigs were more important to
them than people. They loved wealth more than they loved
the reclamation of a human soul. So is it often true today. The
world stands on trial today before the love of Jesus.

The world stands on trial before the cross of Jesus. Very
early one Easter Sunday morning a drunk man came reeling
up to a taxicab in Los Angeles and asked to be taken to the
sunrise service in the Hollywood Bowl. The taxi driver looked
at the man in amazement. "You want to go to the sunrise
service?" he said. "Yes," replied the drunk man. Fearing that
the man would create a scene if he got there, the taxi driver
said to him: "Bud, you're not going, and I'll tell you why.
You've got to carry a cross to go out there, and you aren't
carrying any cross!" One gets the impression, even when he
looks at the people who are in churches, that not many of the
followers of Jesus are carrying a cross that is costing them
very much. The world is on trial today before the cross of
Jesus.

But notice the last two words of the text. They make all
the difference in the world. They turn apprehension into
hope. For the text reads, "We must all appear before the
judgment seat *of Christ.*" He makes the difference. He turns
anguish into joy. He is our Advocate. And he came that we
might have life, not death.

During the war in Korea I was sent, at the invitation of the chief of chaplains of the Air Force, to preach to the boys overseas. I told them that if they would give me the names of their parents, when I returned home I would write to them to say I had seen their son in Korea. In response to those letters to the parents I received some of the most beautiful letters I have ever received in all my life. So many of them invited me to visit them if I was ever in their part of the country. Three of them said it in almost the same way, "You will always be welcome in our home because you met our son in Korea."

Not Christ, but the world, is on trial today. We all stand condemned before the righteousness of God. But this is the message of the cross: We will always be welcome in God's sight when we come at the invitation of his Son. No more do we need to stand condemned before the bar of our own conscience. No more do we need to fear the judgments of God. He has provided for us an advocate. He pleads our case. He secures our pardon. He sets us free. He sends us out into a world where men by their sins are condemned to know bitterness and fear, shame and remorse, hatred and strife, to say that we do not have to wait until we get to heaven to claim the promise; even in this life we can begin to know the joy of the assurance, "There is therefore now no condemnation to them which are in Christ Jesus" (Rom. 8:1). He who is our Judge is also the Father of our Lord, Jesus Christ. We cannot stand before him in our own righteousness. But we can ask his pardon and help and "come boldly unto the throne of grace, that we may obtain mercy, and find grace to help in time of need" (Heb. 4:16)—because we know his Son.

15

Nails for the Master Carpenter's Hand

ISAIAH 22:23

ANYONE WHO READS the book of Isaiah is struck by the wonderful imagination of the prophet. When he wants to warn some of the leaders of Israel of the consequences of their evil acts, he tells them there is no bed into which they can jump and pull the covers up over their heads to hide from the judgments of God, "for the bed is shorter than that a man can stretch himself on it: and the covering narrower than that a man can wrap himself in it" (Isa. 28:20). When he wants to predict the exile of the wicked treasurer Shebna, he pictures God as a cosmic ballplayer and says, "He will surely violently turn and toss thee like a ball into a large country" (22:18). And when he wants to picture the coronation of Eliakim, the son of Hilkiah, he conceives of God as a cosmic carpenter who says, "I will fasten him as a nail in a sure place" (22:23).

This would seem like an unflattering thing to say about a king, for if there is anything commonplace in this world, surely it is a nail. And yet nails are exceedingly important. Nails help to hold the roofs over our heads. Nails help to hold the floors beneath our feet. They even help to hold the soles on our shoes. Without nails the erection of modern buildings would practically be impossible. Much of modern progress would be hampered, and even halted, if suddenly there were no nails for carpenters to use. Even in Isaiah's day nails must have played an important part in the building trade. It was a significant thing, therefore, to say of Eliakim, "I will fasten him as a nail in a sure place."

But the text reminds us of one greater than Eliakim. One cannot ponder this text without being reminded almost immediately that Jesus knew about nails. He knew about nails, in the first place, because as a youth he worked as a carpenter by Joseph's side. Perhaps it was an actual incident in which someone had engaged Joseph and Jesus to build a building, and had then run out of funds before the building was completed, to which Jesus referred when he said, "Which of you, intending to build a tower, sitteth not down first, and counteth the cost, whether he have sufficient to finish it? Lest haply, after he hath laid the foundation, and is not able to finish it, all that behold it begin to mock him" (Luke 14:28–29). When he talked about heaven, Jesus pictured his role as that of a builder, for he said, "In my Father's house are many mansions. . . . I go to prepare a place for you" (John 14:2). Surely it was his experience as a carpenter that led him to couch his teaching in such terms as these.

The famous British clergyman and poet, G. A. Studdert-Kennedy, has envisioned this phase of Jesus' earthly life by asking:

> I wonder what he charged for chairs at Nazareth.
> And did men try to beat him down
> And boast about it in the town—
> "I bought it cheap for half-a-crown
>   From that mad Carpenter?"

And did they promise and not pay,
Put it off to another day;
O, did they break his heart that way,
  My Lord, the Carpenter?

I wonder did he have bad debts,
And did he know my fears and frets?
The gospel writer here forgets
  To tell about the Carpenter.

But that's just what I want to know.
Ah! Christ in glory, here below
Men cheat and lie to one another so;
  It's hard to be a carpenter.[7]

But he did know about the lying and the cheating. He did know about the sins of men. He had to bring healing insight to an immoral Samaritan woman and to a woman taken in adultery. He knew about the selfish avarice of a Zacchaeus. He had to deal with the selfish ambition of the disciples who wanted chief places in his kingdom. He had to deal with the vindictiveness of the Pharisees, the deception of Judas, and the denial of Peter. "He knew what was in man" (John 2:25). He knew that man alone is insufficient to cope with sin. Therefore, in the second place, Jesus knew about nails because as the Saviour of the world, taking upon his sinless heart the sins of mankind, he felt nails being driven by cruel men through the living flesh of his own hands and feet as they nailed him to a cross.

When Jesus came to Golgotha they hanged Him on a tree,
They drave great nails through hands and feet, and made a
  Calvary;

---

[7] "The Carpenter," *1000 Quotable Poems* (Chicago: Willett, Clark and Co., 1937), p. 13.

They crowned Him with a crown of thorns, red were His wounds
    and deep,
For those were crude and cruel days, and human flesh was cheap.[8]

We cannot begin to imagine the agony through which
Jesus must have gone as he hung upon the cross. The pain
must have licked up his arms and legs like living flame as the
weight of his body pulled against the fresh wounds in his
flesh. The wonder is that he could get his teeth unclenched
at all for sheer pain, but the greater wonder is that when he
did speak it was to pray for the very ones who had put him
there.

The nails that held Jesus to the cross have long since been
withdrawn. They have been covered by the shifting sands of
the Middle East, or, more likely, have eroded back to the
elements from which they were made. It is better so. If they
were still in existence, men would encase them in glass and
claim they had efficacy for healing in themselves.

Those nails are gone. There is a sense now in which we are
the nails. Either we are the nails by which he builds his
kingdom, or, by our indifference and sins, we are the nails
by which sinful men still seek to impale him to a cross.

Have you ever thought that a nail is almost a perfect example of the truth that he that loseth his life shall find it?
When a nail is used for the purpose for which a nail is made,
when it is embedded in wood to hold something together, it
is protected from the elements and is kept almost indefinitely
in its original state. But let it be dropped carelessly on the
ground, and overnight it begins to rust and becomes a hazard
to whoever may walk near it. I have in my possession an old
hand-wrought nail that was used to build a house in Alexan-

---

[8] G. A. Studdert-Kennedy, "Indifference," *The Sorrows of God* (New York:
George H. Doran Company, 1924), p. 38.

dria, Virginia, over a hundred years ago. When the house was dismantled, the nail was found to be in as good a condition as it was when it was first pounded into place by some blacksmith's hammer.

When a life, however humble, gives itself for the purpose for which life is made, when it is embedded in the Christian faith and purpose and fellowship, its witness for God is kept shiny and bright through the years. But let it live to itself, let it be exposed to the corrosive acids of self-will, and its witness soon becomes tarnished, and its influence becomes a hazard to whoever may try to follow its example.

Amos Kendall served as postmaster general under two presidents, Andrew Jackson and Martin Van Buren. Though not at the time a professing Christian, he gave the property and a considerable sum of money for the erection of the Calvary Baptist Church of Washington, D.C., on the condition that the church would maintain two kinds of membership: membership in the church by profession of faith and baptism, and membership in the congregation on the basis of a promise to contribute regularly to the work of the church. He himself joined as a member of the congregation.

He must have been proud of his influence. After all, he, a prominent public figure, had given most of the money for the erection of a church. But one day a woman went to see him to say: "My son died without accepting Christ as his personal Saviour. If that means he is eternally lost, it is your fault, because every time we talked to him about surrendering his life to Christ he always gave as his excuse for not doing so, 'Amos Kendall is a good man. He doesn't need to be a professing Christian. Why should I?'" This so moved Amos Kendall that, as an old man, he professed his faith in Christ, and was baptized in the baptistry of the old E Street Baptist Church. Later he gave his witness at a meeting for men, and over twenty men came forward to profess their faith in Christ or to rededicate their lives to his service. The loyalty to which he had given himself made his life count.

So long as he insisted on serving God on his own terms Amos Kendall's influence, in one instance at least, was exactly the opposite to what he thought it would be. When he was willing to accept the Christian faith on God's terms for his life, and became a witnessing member of a Christian church, then his influence led several men to a new or deeper commitment to the kingdom of God.

To let ourselves be used for the purposes of God, however hard the blows of discipline and testing may fall upon us, is to be driven into the security of his love. When by faith we put our lives into the Master's hands, he does fasten them in a sure place. In John 10:27–28 he says, "My sheep hear my voice, and I know them, and they follow me: and I give unto them eternal life; and they shall never perish, neither shall any man pluck them out of my hand." Then he says, "My Father, which gave them me, is greater than all; and no man is able to pluck them out of my Father's hand." And there is no danger of the hands coming apart, for he goes on to say, "I and my Father are one." There can be no surer place than that in which to place our lives. That security cannot possibly fail.

Therefore, let us place our lives at the Master's disposal. For either by faith and commitment we become the nails by which Christ seeks to build his kingdom, or by our indifference and self-will we become the nails by which sinful men seek, as the author of Hebrews so terrifyingly puts it, to "crucify to themselves the Son of God afresh" (6:6). Let us, then, become the nails that are placed in, and not through, his hands. He will use us to build his purposes in the world. He will fasten us in a sure place.

The hands of Christ
   Seem very frail
For they were broken
   By a nail.

But only they
   Reach Heaven at last
Whom these frail, broken
   Hands hold fast.[9]

[9] John Richard Moreland, "His Hands," *The Sea and April* (New York: James T. White & Co., 1928), p. 60. Used by permission.

16

Easter's Threefold Victory

1 CORINTHIANS 15:20

A YOUNG MAN STOOD for the first time on the rim of the Grand Canyon in Arizona. As he looked down into the cavernous depths of that tremendous canyon, carved out of the soil of Arizona by millions of years of erosion as the Colorado River washed away billions and billions of tons of silt, he turned to a companion and said, "Something must have happened here."

That is surely one of the greatest understatements of all time. As one looks at the consequences in history of the resurrection of Jesus, he realizes something of the enormity of the event that happened at Joseph of Arimathea's tomb on the first Easter morning. Something happened there to turn the way of Jesus from a lost cause into a living gospel. Something happened there to turn the disciples from cringing cowards into flaming evangelists. Something happened there that turned Jesus from a dead Messiah into the living Lord of the church. Something happened there that has turned darkness into light, despair into hope, sorrow into joy for millions and millions of Christian believers. Something happened there that underscored the truth of Jesus' words, "I am the resurrection, and the life: he that believeth in me, though he were dead, yet shall he live: and whosoever liveth and believeth

114

in me shall never die" (John 11:25–26). Indeed, something did happen!

Something happened at that empty tomb that split history in two. For if Jesus had not been raised from the dead, we would not now be numbering our years from the approximate date of his birth. If there had been no resurrection, there would have been no New Testament. If there had been no resurrection, there would have been no Christian church. If there had been no resurrection, there would have been no Christian gospel to shed its light across two thousand years of history. The resurrection was so paramount in Paul's thinking that he could say, "If in this life only we have hope in Christ, we are of all men most miserable. But now is Christ risen from the dead. . . . Therefore, my beloved brethren, be ye stedfast, unmoveable, always abounding in the work of the Lord, forasmuch as ye know that your labour is not in vain in the Lord" (1 Cor. 15:19–20, 58). And again, "If thou shalt confess with thy mouth the Lord Jesus, and shalt believe in thine heart that God hath raised him from the dead, thou shalt be saved" (Rom. 10:9).

But what does Easter mean? What is the significance of this event? Its significance is boundless, timeless. It means God is not dead. It means the grave is not the end of man's hopes. It means man is not a cosmic accident to be discarded like a broken toy at death. It means man is not made for a mere threescore years and ten. He must take all eternity into account. It means we are made for more than eating and drinking. We are made for fellowship with God—a fellowship as timeless as God is timeless. It means that the resurrection that happened so silently, and that was known at first by only a few, has become history's most world-shaking event. If Easter is true, sinners had better get right with God —or tremble. If Easter is true, neither judgment nor the joy of faith is limited to this life; one has all eternity to live under the judgment of God or to receive his joy.

This, and much more, Easter means. Let me now, out of all its cosmic significance, select three of its meanings.

In the first place, Easter is the story of a kingdom an empire could not overthrow. Rome was the dominant power in the world of Jesus' day. Rome's armies were everywhere. Rome's word was law. And while it boasted of its law, it was not above taking the law into its own hands if it felt it was necessary to do so to maintain its power. If one of its emissaries wanted to kill all the male babies under two years of age in Bethlehem, who was there to stop him? If one of its armies wanted to wipe out the village of Sepphoris near Nazareth, hanging every male inhabitant on a cross because some of them had insurrected and Rome wanted to give the world an object lesson, who was there to prevent it? With military might like that behind him, a ruler has the power of life and death in his hands. Pilate could look at Jesus and say, "Speakest thou not unto me? knowest thou not that I have the power to crucify thee, and have power to release thee?" (John 19:10). How futile the words of Jesus must have sounded to a man like Pilate! "My kingdom is not of this world: if my kingdom were of this world, then would my servants fight. . . . To this end was I born, and for this cause came I into the world, that I should bear witness unto the truth. Every one that is of the truth heareth my voice" (John 18:36–37).

This didn't make sense to Pilate, any more than it makes sense to millions of people today. Truth? What kind of a basis is that on which to build a kingdom? Armies, yes. Violence and the threat of violence, yes. Political intrigue and deceit, yes. Jesus once said of Satan that he was a murderer and the father of lies. There you have the two great diabolical forces, violence and deceit, on which so many empires have sought to build themselves. No wonder Pilate asked, in evident contempt, "What is truth?" But Jesus went on believing in the power of love and truth to prevail where brute force is bound to fail, and that the truth that was in him would become incorporated in a fellowship against which the gates of hell cannot prevail.

Pilate had no way of knowing that the resurrection would change everything. He could not foresee an event that would turn the disciples from cringing cowards into flaming evangelists. He could not foresee an event that would cause the disciples to put forth such tendrils of faith that not even Rome, with all its ruthless cruelty, could cut away the Christian movement from the arbor of that ancient world. And yet Rome is now buried in history books and the Christian cause of which Pilate was so contemptuous is still alive.

Rome was not the last great power to underestimate the vitality of Jesus. Hitler made that mistake. Hitler was contemptuous of the church, but the church has outlived Hitler. Russia seems to be learning the same lesson. When Russia was getting its propaganda for atheism into high gear, one of the great churches in Moscow was taken over and made into a science museum. From the dome of the church a great pendulum was hung. As it moved back and forth over the course of a twenty-four hour period, it would veer in the direction in which the earth was rotating. The guide would point out to visitors the principle of the pendulum, and then he would say: "For centuries the church taught that the world was flat. This pendulum shows you that the church lied." Sometimes when there were non-Russians in the group, the guide would turn to them and slyly remark, "Perhaps your church will be a good place to hang a pendulum."

But the swinging pendulum has not emptied all the

churches of Russia, for there are thousands of Russian people who know that Communist propaganda, for all its cleverness, cannot give a satisfying answer to the question, "From where do the laws come that govern the movements of the earth and the pendulum?" And there are millions of people in the world who know that all the material blessings in the world cannot cleanse a guilty heart or comfort a broken one. Only God can do that—the God who revealed himself through his Son, through his matchless life, through his death on a cross, through his wonderful resurrection from the dead. Christ still lives to reveal himself through the experience and vitality of the Christian fellowship. And while the church itself often needs purging, and while the church as we know it is not identical with the kingdom of God, nevertheless the church is trying through its faith, its worship, its fellowship, its witness, to incorporate in the life of the world that which Jesus had in mind when he talked about the kingdom of God. Rome is gone; the church remains. Easter is the story of a kingdom an empire could not overthrow.

In the second place, Easter is the story of a love hate could not defeat.

Think of the hate that was in the world into which Jesus was born. Almost everybody hated someone else. The Jews hated the Samaritans, the Samaritans hated the Jews. Jews and Samaritans alike hated the Romans, and the Romans hated them back. Pharisees hated the Herodians; taxpayers hated the publicans. Hate was so dominant in the thinking of his people that all Jesus had to do was to stand up in the synagogue in Nazareth and say, "There were many lepers in Israel in the time of Isaiah the prophet; and none of them was cleansed, saving Naaman the Syrian"; and his fellow countrymen were so incensed they took Jesus to the edge of the town and were going to throw him over a cliff. Yet in that kind of a world he taught love and forgiveness. In that kind of a world he refused to hate. If ever hate had a field day, it did at Calvary. Men mocked him, struck him, spit on him, lashed his back. They nailed him on a tree, but even then, with every nerve of his body racked with pain, he prayed, "Father, forgive them; for they know not what they do" (Luke 23:34).

We still live in a world of hate. The Jews now hate the Arabs, and the Arabs hate the Jews. There are millions of people in the world who now hate the United States. The Communists hate everyone who is not a Communist. I suppose the world has never known such a large-scale deliberate effort to foment hate as we have seen in our day. When the first Baptist leaders went into Russia after the war, nobody, not even the Baptist people, could believe them when they said America wants peace. "That is not true," the people would say; "we know better." One of the Baptist leaders from America came to the conclusion the most important thing he could do on the trip was to say over and over again: "America wants peace. Her people want peace. They pray for peace. The President of the United States wants peace." When they felt they could believe him, many Russians wept for sheer joy.

I hardly need to point out that there is plenty of hatred here in our own country. But the love of Christ is not dead. The churches have not perfectly reflected his love, but they do reach out arms of missionary love to the ends of the earth. When hate had done its worst at Calvary, the love of God still spoke. When it seemed to be silenced in the tomb, it broke forth to say again in love, "Go ye therefore, and teach all nations, baptizing them in the name of the Father, and of the Son, and of the Holy Ghost" (Matt. 28:19). If we stand with Christ, even though the world hate us, love will have its

Easter, for not even death can prevent God from crowning both us and our efforts with glory and honor.

But, greatest of all, Easter is the story of a life death could not destroy.

It was not just the influence of Jesus that lived on. That can be said of Aristotle and Shakespeare. It was not just his truth that lived on. That can be said of Galileo and Newton. It was Jesus who lived on. We can believe him when he says, "Because I live, you also shall live."

During the war a young soldier came into my office to tell me he thought he would soon be sent overseas. He knew the danger into which he would be going. He said, "I don't think I would mind going quite so much if I could really be sure that if I didn't come back that wouldn't be the end of me."

I admitted I could not prove life after death the way a chemist can prove that water is made up of hydrogen and oxygen. But I asked him if he knew about Stradivarius violins. He said he did. So I said: "Can you imagine Stradivari making as beautiful a violin as human hands can make, working until every muscle of his back must have ached and until his eyes must have smarted from looking so steadily at his work, only to have someone play a few tunes on it, and then taking it back and smashing it against his workbench? That doesn't make sense. And while I say it reverently, I don't think it makes sense to think that God would go to all the trouble to create a human personality, a human soul, and then after a few short years take it back to smash it forever against the workbench of the universe. That is not the kind of a God in whom Jesus taught us to believe."

Then I said: "But my real reason for believing that if you did not come back in the flesh that would not be the end of you is this. I believe you cannot explain the Christian church apart from the resurrection of Jesus. It was not his teachings, it was not his influence, as powerful as those were, that sent the disciples out to die for their faith. It was their assurance that Jesus was alive again and one day they would see him face to face."

Without Easter Jesus' words in John 14:2, "I go to prepare a place for you," are beautiful prose. Because of Easter they become a blessed promise. Without Easter every human aspiration and yearning would be swallowed up by death. Because of Easter death itself is swallowed up in victory. Without Easter we would have every reason to despair. "But now is Christ risen from the dead" (1 Cor. 15:20). "Therefore . . . be ye stedfast, unmoveable, always abounding in the work of the Lord, forasmuch as ye know that your labour is not in vain in the Lord" (1 Cor. 15:58). For Easter is the story of a kingdom empires cannot overthrow, a love hate cannot defeat, and life that death cannot destroy. Let us sing, Hallelujah!

17

Life's Most Dangerous Prayer

LUKE 4:34

WE HAVE LOOKED at messages from the life and teachings of Jesus. Now what do we do about them? This is important to ask, because three times in the course of the Bible we run across a phrase that represents the attitude of millions of people, most of them decent, law-abiding citizens; and yet this attitude has done as much, if not more, to hinder the progress of the kingdom of God on earth as almost anything else one could mention. The phrase is, "Let me alone," or "Let us alone." This is a prayer which, if it were answered, would denude the world of hope and would result in the direst fate that could possibly befall mankind.

The first time we run across this phrase we find it in Exodus 14:12 in the experience of the children of Israel after they have crossed through the Red Sea under the leadership of Moses. Life in the desert is hard, food is scarce, the future is uncertain. Finally, in a mood of panic, the people complain to Moses, saying, "Is this not the word that we did tell thee in Egypt, saying, Let us alone, that we may serve the Egyptians? For it had been better for us to serve the Egyptians, than that we should die in the wilderness."

People's memories are short. Sometimes this is a good thing. How unbearable life would be if we continued to remember all the slights, real or imagined, that have been done to us. In this case, however, it was tragic. They were forgetting that back in Egypt they could not call body or soul their own. They were forgetting the bricks they had to make without straw. They were forgetting the times when they had had to grub in the fields for stubble, and were required to turn out as many bricks under those conditions as when the straw had been provided. They were forgetting the sting of the taskmaster's whip when they failed to turn out the required number of bricks. All this was becoming a dim memory. Now they saw only the hardships of the present. And so in their complaining mood they said, "Is this not the word that we did tell thee in Egypt, saying, Let us alone, that we may serve the Egyptians?"

The second time we run across this phrase it is with a good deal more justification. Job is almost at the end of his rope. He has taken just about all he can stand. His body is worn down by illness; his spirit is worn down by the incessant arguments of his friends. Finally, in exhaustion and despair, he lifts his eyes to heaven and, in Job 10:20, says to the Lord: "Are not my days few? cease then, and let me alone, that I may take comfort a little." If his prayer had been answered, Job never would have been restored to health, and the latter end of Job would never have been blessed "more than his beginning."

The third time we hear this phrase, in Luke 4:34, it is spoken in the synagogue in Nazareth. Jesus has come to the synagogue to worship and teach. A man who is described as having the spirit of an unclean devil cries out to Jesus: "Let us alone; what have we to do with thee, thou Jesus of Nazareth? . . . I know thee who thou art; the Holy One of

God." Thus, he sought to hang on to his unclean spirit and to forestall the cleansing he knew Jesus was able to give.

There you have the three statements: "Let us alone, that we may serve the Egyptians." "Let me alone, that I may take comfort a little." "Let us alone; what have we to do with thee, thou Jesus of Nazareth?"

One hardly needs to point out that each of these statements has its counterpart today. There are those, for example, who say, "Let us alone that we may serve the world, for it had been better that we should die in our sins than that we should fail to be popular or to enjoy the pleasures and plaudits of the world."

As suggested in an earlier chapter, the people who take this attitude are traveling under two gross misconceptions. The first is that the pleasures of sin are all they advertise themselves to be; and they never are. Sin promises one thing; it delivers quite another. It promises happiness and delivers disillusionment and remorse. It promises hours filled with excitement and delivers an empty life. It promises life and delivers death. In the story of Jesus' temptations, when Satan promises that if Jesus would bow down and worship him he would give him the kingdoms of the world, Satan did not have the world to give. He did not own one square foot of it. "The earth is the Lord's, and the fulness thereof" (Psalm 24:1). If Jesus had bowed down and worshiped Satan, he would have lost his soul and the world as well.

Paul knew this. He wrote, "Satan himself is transformed into an angel of light" (2 Cor. 11:14). He comes dressed in the garb of peace, but sows seeds of conflict and war. He comes wearing the smile of a friend, but his mind is the mind of a scheming fiend. He comes fawning like a friendly dog, but he walks about as a "roaring lion . . . seeking whom he may devour" (1 Peter 5:8).

The author of Ecclesiastes seems to have discovered this. He first started out to get knowledge, to discover that, while education is exceedingly important, without a genuine faith or a moral purpose in one's life education can be vanity. He tried folly, to discover it left a bad taste in his mouth. He is even frank enough to confess he tried alcohol, but instead of solving his problems, it created a new one. He tried getting money, to discover that all his money, and he had a lot, could not buy him happiness. Finally, he tried faith in God, to discover it gave him such peace and happiness he pleads with young people, "Remember now thy Creator in the days of thy youth, while the evil days come not, nor the years draw nigh, when thou shalt say, I have no pleasure in them" (Eccl. 12:1). As he gets to the end of his book, he says, "Let us hear the conclusion of the whole matter: Fear God, and keep his commandments: for this is the whole duty of man" (Eccl. 12:13).

Of course, there is pessimism in his book. He still hadn't seen God in the face of Jesus Christ. We have. Therefore, a Christian ought to be the happiest person on the face of the earth. For this is the second misconception under which people proceed when they feel they must not miss out on the pleasures of this world—they think Christians do not have any fun. There may be some Christians who give that impression, but by and large Christians are the happiest people on the face of the earth, for their pleasures do not leave the bitter taste of remorse after the thrill of the moment has passed. Instead, they collect new dividends of joy every time they remember their Christian joys and pleasures.

A young man once pawned his overcoat to buy a ticket to hear the great Paderewski play the piano. Years later he confessed he had never regretted his act, because every time he remembers the beauty of that concert and the thrill of hearing Paderewski play he gets new pleasure out of the memory. We need to remember that the real pleasures of life are those that God himself has given us. All Satan can do is to try to get us to abuse or misuse them or make them ends in themselves. If we accept them as gifts from God and use them under the direction of the Holy Spirit to build a well-rounded life and to serve God and our fellow men, then, like a young girl who faced privation after the war to serve as a missionary in some of the bombed-out areas of Japan, we too shall be able to say, "Each day for me is a glorious new adventure."

As we indicated, the next cry has a good deal more to justify it, for there are many times when some of us feel like crying out with Job: "Are not my days few? cease then, and let me alone, that I may take comfort a little."

Some people seem to get more than their share of suffering, and all of us have times when we seem to get out of one trouble only to get into another one. We live in a world where one international crisis follows close on the heels of another, so that we live in a constant state of cold war jitters. In our personal lives, we get out of one problem only to get into another, sometimes bigger. Just as we think we are going to get out of debt, illness comes, or the roof springs a leak, or the children go away to college, and we find ourselves more deeply in debt than ever. Or, how often it is true that when one gets to the place where he has saved up a little money, and thinks he can retire and enjoy life, illness or bereavement comes and upsets the entire plan, so that a person is tempted to cry out: "Are not my days few? cease then, and let me alone, that I may take comfort a little." We cry out for some relief from it all.

Some time ago a man with an incurable disease wrote this poem on the hospital wall next to his bed:

The cry of man's anguish went up unto God:
  "Lord, take away pain—
The shadow that darkens the world thou hast made,
  The close-coiling chain
That strangles the heart, the burden that weighs
  On the wings that would soar—
Lord, take away pain from the world thou hast made,
  That it love thee the more!"

But even as he wrote, he already knew the answer, for in the second verse he had written:

Then answered the Lord to the cry of his world:
  "Shall I take away pain
And with it the power of the soul to endure,
  Made strong by the strain?
Shall I take away pity, that knits heart to heart,
  And sacrifice high?
Will ye lose all your heroes that lift from the fire
  White brows to the sky?
Shall I take away love, that redeems with a price
  And smiles at its loss?
Can ye spare from your lives, that would climb unto mine,
  The Christ on his cross?" [10]

No one in his right mind wants to suffer. No normal person enjoys suffering. But if we had no suffering, would we have sympathy? Would we have the dedication of doctors and nurses? Would we have the unselfish concern that suffering calls forth? All of us know that sometimes hours of pain and sorrow can make us more deeply conscious of the presence of God and of our personal need of him than all the cloudless, happy hours in the world.

In some ways the third group presents the most serious

---

[10] "Take Away Pain," *Poems with Power to Strengthen the Soul*, compiled by James Mudge (New York: The Abingdon Press, 1909), p. 160.

problem of all. Their problem is not so much theological as psychological. It is not that they disbelieve Jesus. They just don't want to be bothered, and so they say: "What have we to do with thee, thou Jesus of Nazareth? Let us alone, that we may live our own lives as we ourselves want to live them." Like Pilate they say, "We find no fault in him," then turn around and condemn him to a cross of indifference. Or they say to the church: "What have we to do with thee? Let us alone, that we may not have to listen to your preaching or respond to your calls for loyalty and help." It is not that they disbelieve in the church. Most of them would not want to live in a community in which there was no church. They just don't want to be bothered. And so, rather than surrender their wills to the will of Christ, rather than offer their lives and talents to the work of his kingdom, they go on their own selfish way, not wanting to be bothered by those who need their example and help.

So when the church needs those without whose loyalty and support it cannot do its work in the world, they are conspicuous by their absence. When the Lord needs a witness that will give help to some individual or situation, they are too busy, or preoccupied, or self-righteous, or complacent, or lazy to respond. Many of them think of themselves as pretty decent, upright sort of people, and in a moral sense they may be. But they deny the kingdom of God the loyalty and service it needs if God is to minister through his church to a sinful and needy world.

In this day and age it is not easy to frighten people into righteousness, and one would not wish to do so if he could. That is not the best motivation to get committed lives. Nevertheless, to those who adopt an attitude of hostility or indifference and who continue to say, "Let us alone; what have we to do with thee, thou Jesus of Nazareth?" it needs to be said that the day may come when God will grant them their wish.

The New Testament speaks clearly at this point. It does not represent the righteousness of God as a wishy-washy thing. It does not present the opposite of grace as merely having no grace, but as disgrace, the actual disfavor of God. It tells of those for whom the door is shut, and they may not enter. And in the words not of a ranting preacher, but of Jesus himself, it says, "There shall be weeping and gnashing of teeth" (Matt. 8:12). For there will be those who will discover that the very worst thing that could happen to us would be for God to let us alone. Without his help we could not live a single day. Without his grace we could not face eternity with any hope or confidence. Many there are who have cried, "Let me alone," who, when they enter the valley of the shadow of death, will desperately need God's presence and help, only to find he has at long last honored their lifelong prayer, and has no other alternative. For he will not violate their freedom to reject him if that is what they choose, but grant their wish and let them alone to think through all eternity of the joy they might have known and of the wasted lives they have lived when they could have lived and been used to the glory of God.

This also needs to be said: As long as we live, God never will be guilty of adopting a "let me alone" attitude toward us. From the beginning to the end, the Bible presents a God who "neither slumbers nor sleeps"; a God who says, "Whosoever will may come"; a God who is never too busy to answer prayer, never too preoccupied to miss the fall even of the smallest sparrow. When we need him, he is there. When we call upon him, he will answer, not always in the way we think he should, but in terms of his own infinite love and wisdom.

A crippled boy, bitter because of his handicapped condition, began to study psychology to try to live with his bitterness. One day he met a radiant Christian who had the faith he lacked and wanted so much to have. He asked her how she got it. She said, "Much of it through prayer." He began to drop into a church for meditation and prayer. It did not happen overnight, but as he exposed his heart and mind to the indwelling presence of God, the miracle took place. God broke through into his life, and he became a transformed person who today is one of the most influential Christian laymen in his community. When he turned to God in his need, God did not say, "Let me alone," but responded with transforming power. And to a world that so often shrugs its shoulders and says to God, "Let me alone," God still speaks through the cross to a restless, searching, needy, unhappy world: "Come unto me, all ye that labour and are heavy laden, and I will give you rest. Take my yoke upon you, and learn of me; for I am meek and lowly in heart: and ye shall find rest unto your souls" (Matt. 11:28–29).